THE INTERPERSONAL
NEUROBIOLOGY OF PLAY

THE INTERPERSONAL NEUROBIOLOGY OF PLAY

Brain-Building Interventions for Emotional Well-Being

THERESA A. KESTLY

W. W. Norton & Company
New York • London

Quoted Material, Chapters 2 & 5, Reprinted by permission of the publisher from *The First Relationship: Infant and Mother*, with a new introduction by Daniel N. Stern, pp. 16, 18–19, 21–22, 130, Cambridge, Mass.: Harvard University Press, Copyright © 2002 by the President and Fellows of Harvard College, Copyright © 1977 by Daniel N. Stern.

Copyright © 2014 by Theresa A. Kestly

All rights reserved
Printed in the United States of America
First Edition

For information about permission to reproduce selections from this book, write to Permissions, W. W. Norton & Company, Inc., 500 Fifth Avenue, New York, NY 10110

For information about special discounts for bulk purchases, please contact W. W. Norton Special Sales at specialsales@wwnorton.com or 800-233-4830

Manufacturing by Quad Graphics Fairfield
Production manager: Leeann Graham

Library of Congress Cataloging-in-Publication Data

Kestly, Theresa A., author.
   The interpersonal neurobiology of play : brain-building interventions for emotional well-being / Theresa A. Kestly ; foreword by Bonnie Badenoch. — First edition.
       p. ; cm. — (Norton series on interpersonal neurobiology)
   Includes bibliographical references and index.
   ISBN 978-0-393-70749-6 (hardcover)
   I. Title.   II. Series: Norton series on interpersonal neurobiology.
   [DNLM: 1. Child.   2. Play Therapy.   3. Brain—physiology.
4. Neurobiology.   WS 350.4]
RJ505.P6
618.92'891653—dc23   2014019354

ISBN: 978-0-393-70749-6

W. W. Norton & Company, Inc., 500 Fifth Avenue, New York, N.Y. 10110
www.wwnorton.com
W. W. Norton & Company Ltd., 15 Carlisle, London W1D 3BS

2 3 4 5 6 7 8 9 0

For my daughter
Catherine Wynona

CONTENTS

Contents

ACKNOWLEDGMENTS

In writing this book I have come to a much deeper understanding of just how important play is to me in a number of different ways. More than once, when I felt stuck about what to write next or how to articulate an idea, I found that if I could enter into a playful attitude with my writing, it was usually quite helpful. For a long time I have used journaling for the purpose of personal growth, but as I was writing this book, I began to practice more consistently a writing technique I learned in a workshop with Natalie Goldberg, author of *Writing Down the Bones.* Before we gathered for the workshop, Natalie instructed us to bring a pen that "writes really fast"—one where the tip just glides over the paper (no obstructions!) and any old paper—not expensive bound journaling books where we might be afraid to mess them up with words that might not come out in polished, finished form. When we began, Natalie asked us to write continuously about a specific topic for a certain period of time without stopping to think—"just keep writing every word that comes to you—no editing." Her instructions sounded open and nonthreatening to me, and so I began with a playful attitude. I loved it, and I was surprised by the ideas that began to flow more freely. Putting into practice what I learned from Natalie when I began writing this book, I found myself often leaving my computer to pick up pen and paper to write playfully—playing with the words and opening up new thoughts and ideas. It just about always helped me to get back on track. So first, I want to thank Natalie for the practice of open, playful writing.

During this book project, I developed a deep appreciation for the amazing staff at Norton, especially Deborah Malmud for her clear focus, direction, and support of this project. Kathryn Moyer, Benjamin Yarling, Sophie Hagen, Sara Peterson and Margaret Ryan were also very helpful, kind, and patient, beyond what anyone could expect, with my endless questions and all the details involved in completing this book.

I am deeply grateful for Bonnie Badenoch's wisdom, encouragement and support throughout this entire writing project. She read the whole manuscript as I was writing it, and she gave me invaluable feedback every step of the way. A heartfelt thanks goes to Patty Mourant, colleague and friend, for reading every chapter and giving me practical feedback from her clinical expertise. To Mary Thelma Brainard, greatly valued colleague, I just want to say thanks for the many long discussions about play and how it is intertwined with our clinical work.

As I wrote, I often thought about my very first playmates, 3 brothers—Ron, David and John, and 2 sisters—Lois and Donna. We grew up in a time before television or electronic games, when our biggest sources of entertainment were hours of sledding down the hill behind our home, family play nights when my mother would make popcorn and my father would engage us in an evening of hide-and-seek, the rough and tumble play of learning how to be siblings, playing "dolls" with my sisters, snow forts, tree houses, a backyard sandbox, a miniature sand box at Sunday school where we acted out Bible stories, arts and crafts of our own design, and anything else we could dream up to occupy our leisure time. We had a lot of serious moments too when we were growing up. There were plenty of chores, but we could always count on playtime when we were finished. It was a pattern of play balanced with meaningful work, a pattern that began early and, so far, has lasted a lifetime. This became so clear to me recently, when my siblings and I came together for a family reunion. I realized that we could still play together—making puzzles, telling jokes on one another, laughing a lot, sharing family stories, and just having fun. We also could still share the work entailed in spending a week together in my home—the cooking, the cleanup and all the other mundane tasks associated with daily life. I am grateful for my family of origin, and I feel especially lucky that I now have the miniature sand tray from my Sunday school where I first played in the sand to tell stories when I was just 6 years old. I have the sand tray because my siblings went to a great deal of trouble to get it for me and to transport it from Pennsylvania to New Mexico where I now have it in my teaching studio.

Much thanks goes to my daughter, and now also my grandchildren, for teaching me a lot more about play. We have engaged in a lot of old-fashioned play together, but they also introduced me to the joys of electronic games, the wonders of paid-for play, Legos, and a host of other interesting options. No matter the form, play seems generally to link us in the relationships we so much want and need.

This book could never have been written without the insight I gained from the patients who came to me for therapy, the students who came to learn about the sand tray, and my teachers, especially my third grade teacher, Mrs. Sargent, who believed I could write. I am also grateful for my mentor, Ross Mooney, from Ohio State University, who taught me how to think from a living systems perspective where our relationships with one another are core.

Finally, and importantly, I want to thank David Kestly, my husband for his full support and encouragement of this long and time-consuming project. Hopefully, we will soon make up for the playtime that, I must confess, I have too often put "on hold" over the past few years. I am grateful for David's patience and not giving up on the prospects for play.

FOREWORD

by Bonnie Badenoch

Theresa Kestly is a powerful advocate for the wisdom and power of play. As our culture continues to devalue this essential joyous activity, she is an important voice, weaving both neuroscience and story into a compelling tapestry in support of her conviction of play's deep and ongoing value in our lives, and particularly in the lives of our children. Her narratives bring the principles to life as though we were with her in the playroom, while her profound kindness and respect for parents and their children infuses every page.

Her love of play and intuitive sense of its life-giving qualities was nourished by her own early experiences. Theresa was raised in pre-TV times, which meant lots of outdoor play in a small community where everyone felt safe enough not to lock their doors. There were lots of neighborhood children and ample play space in multiple neighborhood yards and school playgrounds. Kestly grew up believing that play was the natural reward after family chores and responsibilities were finished. To find in recent times that some schools are eliminating recess and building new facilities without playgrounds has created a feeling of urgency in her to draw together the resources that help us to understand the injury this is doing our young ones.

Drawing on her 27 years of playing with children as a therapist, Kestly begins with the question she has so often heard from parents of the young ones brought to her playroom—"How can 'just playing' help?" She offers the emerging discoveries of neuroscience to guide the development of our understanding of the ways that play shapes children's brains in the direction of relational health, expanding cognitive capacity, and creativity. Beyond and within that is the celebration of pure joy, for no reason, that is at the core of playfulness. As she points out, in our speedy, achievement-oriented, left-hemisphere culture, "for no reason" means worthless, so the essential life-giving quality of play can go unfelt and undervalued by society at large.

At the beginning of the book and throughout, Kestly focuses on the interpersonal nature of play. The warm, curious, nonjudgmental presence of the play therapist provides the nurturing soil in which children can move more deeply within their minds, hearts, and bodies to bring forward the implicit memories of what has wounded them. As these places of fear or pain are held in the safety of the play relationship, they begin to change their felt sense and integrate in a different way. By working at this depth, as the pain and fear are resolved, behaviors shift as well. Kestly is such an advocate for seeing children's behavior as adaptive protections these young ones have developed in response to the interpersonal challenges around them. When they are given the opportunity to explore the wounds beneath the behavior, their natural need and longing for warm attachments and more harmonious relationships begins to emerge.

In the first half of her book, Kestly grounds this viewpoint in the discoveries of neuroscience, particularly the work of Stephen Porges (the nervous system in play), Jaak Panksepp (the PLAY system as one of our inborn emotional/motivational networks), Daniel Siegel (attachment, neuroplasticity, and neural integration), and Iain McGilchrist (the essential relationship between the two hemispheres). All of these researchers and theoreticians give the interpersonal relationship an important place in healing. With Kestly, the centrality of relationship is made concrete by both her clear articulation of the theory and the stories that embody this. One of the beauties of her approach is that she moves in a spiral pattern, revisiting the main themes of safety, connection, play, neural integration, and the right-centric viewpoint over and over, giving us time and support to deeply internalize the ways these complex theories might move into practice.

Building on this secure foundation, when we come to Part II of the book—which is focused more deliberately on practical applications—we have already developed a good deal of comfort with the interface between theory and practice. She begins by speaking with us about the play sanctuaries that Plato wrote about, suggesting that the therapist him/herself may now be the sanctuary that children need. She goes on to develop possible ways a play space may be set up as a relationally safe and inviting holding environment for all who come. This beautiful evocation of the play space as a reflection of the therapist's intention provides such strong encouragement and support for us to mindfully prepare the environment.

As we settle into the space, she moves on to talk about the collaborative relationship itself, with such profound respect for young ones and their capacity to heal. From there, the rest of the book opens out into some ways we might be with our young ones— through storytelling, in the sand, with the support of art, and even with Legos.

The last chapter is tour-de-force argument revisiting the importance of play—as an essential reflection of what it is to be human— through the lifespan. She speaks to the state of our culture at this point, and all that is at risk when we abandon this essential activity in favor of more academics, structured sports, and other forms that limit the full expression of this inborn urge. I believe it would be wonderful to print a million copies of this chapter and airdrop them all over the western world. Iain McGilchrist, someone to whom Kestly returns again and again, points toward the strong left-shift in western culture as a dehumanizing force that takes us away from our ability to sense one another's humanity with devastating consequences for how our society is organized. He suggests that our brains evolved to work in a certain pattern—the right-mode, the relational in-the-moment perspective, is meant to be in the lead and providing the vision; while the left-mode, perspective, is intended to create systems to manifest this humanitarian vision. We seem to have lost our way, and Kestly is making a vital contribution toward righting the course.

It seems fitting to end this foreword with a story that epitomizes what Theresa brings. Early in her career, she met a young boy who was afraid of leaving his mother's lap, largely nonverbal, and clearly miserable. After a few sessions of no connection, she felt pulled into such a depth of misery that she heard her mind say, "I don't like this boy." It frightened her, new as she was to working with young ones. She somehow felt drawn to attend closely to what she was feeling and realized that this unremitting misery might well be what this boy felt every day. With that, compassion welled up in her, and gradually the therapy took on a different flavor as he opened to her unspoken acceptance. On this foundation, a relationship gradually developed, and as Theresa introduced sand tray into her playroom, this young one began to tell his nonverbal story.

Rarely did he talk about his sand worlds, but his images were consistent, and Theresa could see that it was a powerful vehicle for him to tell his wordless story of how painful it was to live in a very frightening world that was full of danger. He used the vulnerable little rabbits almost every session, and occasionally he would bring in rattlesnakes and other dangerous items. For a long time, there were no humans in any of the sand trays, but finally one day the humans entered the world. As soon as the humans' feet touched the sand, however, the rabbits all darted into their holes that he had so carefully prepared beforehand. Theresa rarely talked while he was building his trays, but this time, she said, "They feel much safer in their holes." He looked at her and said, "They're not really that afraid." One by one, he brought each rabbit out of its hole.

Not long after this tray, other humans came into the sand worlds to feed the animals and to take care of them. Theresa was pretty sure that this boy was well on his path to healing by this time. His mother corroborated her observations. She said that he was doing well at school and making new friends in ways he had never been able to before. Almost without words, in the embrace of this relationship, something changed. In the years since, the explorations and discoveries of neuroscience have begun placing a solid foundation for understanding and sharing with others the enduring power of play, an intersection of science and experience that is expressed beautifully in this book.

INTRODUCTION

As Kenny and I walked toward my play therapy room, his mother said, "Now talk to her today. Don't just play!" He didn't respond. Nor did it seem she expected a response. At that moment, I really wanted to talk to Kenny's mom about the importance of play in helping him deal with the stress of his father's absence. I knew in my heart that play was crucial in his therapy, but that was a long time ago, before the decade of the brain, and I would have been hard-pressed to explain scientifically why play might be our best chance to support Kenny's return to a healthy developmental path. He was just 4 years old, and from our first therapy session, when he and his mom played with clay in my office, Kenny called me the "clay lady." With little apparent concern for his mother's admonishment, he was just eager to get to the playroom.

Inside the playroom with Kenny, I realized that his mom had just put words to a sentiment that seems to run deep in our dominantly left-brain, word-centered society. From that hemisphere's perspective, play is so often seen as trivial, as what children should do only when there is no more important task to be done or words to say. The "just playing" phrase kept ringing in my ears, and I couldn't let it rest. I decided to find out why play is so important from a scientific and theoretical point of view, so I could explain to Kenny's mom, in language she could understand, why he was so eager to play. Over time, the task of explaining the importance of play to parents became easier, and now thankfully, research from a number of different disciplines is helping us put the pieces of the puzzle together. New information is flowing rapidly, especially from the fields of neuroscience and interpersonal neurobiology. We are getting a much better picture of why we need to care about play.

One neuroscientist, Jaak Panksepp (Panksepp & Biven, 2012), describes play as one of the major brain sources of joy, and he says that it is one of the seven motivational systems inherent in our brains when we are born. Play has its own neural circuitry, and when children feel safely connected to others, the circuitry of play is naturally activated.

Panksepp believes that play may be so important that it might even be a wise cultural investment to create play sanctuaries where preschoolers could have opportunities for natural play. Panksepp underscores the importance of exploratory, prosocial play in developing the frontal lobe inhibitory circuitry that helps children (and adults) regulate impulsive primary-process emotional urges. He says, "Abundant early play opportunities may culturally and epigenetically benefit children's happy and empathic BrainMind development for a lifetime" (Panksepp & Biven, 2012, p. 387).

Could play possibly be this important—so important that its effects could last a lifetime? Stuart Brown, M.D., director of The National Institute for Play, believes that its influence is this long-lasting, and that it unlocks human potential at all stages of life. Although most play scholars agree that play is necessary in the neurobiological development of children, Brown (Brown & Vaughn, 2009) draws from research and clinical observations to suggest that play is equally important for the well-being of adults. Similarly, in a formal study of adult development conducted at the Harvard Medical School, Vaillant (2002) concluded that playfulness and creativity were among some of the important factors that determine a retiree's sense of well-being and happiness. Knowing how to play, which often overlaps with being creative, made all the difference, according to the Harvard study, in whether retirees ended up in a sad/sick or a happy/well category. From this prospective longitudinal study, it appears that play abilities have an impact not only on one's emotional well-being but also on physical health as well over the entire lifespan. (A *prospective study* is one in which events are recorded as they happen; in contrast, a retrospective study records past events based on memories.) Lifestyle propensities—one of them being play—turned out to be more important than genetics, wealth, ethnic origins, or other factors in predicting how happy the participants of the study would be in retirement years. Our brains are built to benefit from play no matter what our age.

Given that play seems to be an important factor in aging well, and that it also may have direct impact on helping children develop frontal lobe regulatory and empathic functions, it is helpful that neuroscience is now giving us the foundation we need to take a serious look at why and how we are endowed with play circuitry from the very beginning. We will return shortly to the laboratory work of Panksepp to discover in more detail what is happening in the play circuitry of our genetically inherited motivational systems.

JUST PLAYING?

If Kenny did hear his mother's directive to talk, not just play, it did not deter him from diving into the toys and art materials when he got to the playroom. I could understand his mother's need to have every moment of the therapy count. She was newly divorced and trying to get a degree at the university so that she could support herself and her children. Paying for therapy was a challenge, but she wanted Kenny to work through his anger and sadness about the divorce, and she definitely wanted him to behave better. As we delve into what transpires in Kenny's brain processes, we will be able to understand that the disrupted connection with his father left him with feelings of fear, anger, separation distress, and lack of safety, leading to off-track behaviors. If we could restore his sense of connection and liberate his play circuitry in the safety of the playroom, he might be able to release these feelings and find a way back toward harmony with his mother. We now have research in both animal and human studies to support the idea that children develop self-regulation through play. An additional incentive for Kenny's mom and other parents like her might be the studies that also support a link between self-regulation and academic success. Despite my inability to articulate the "why" of play therapy at that point in time, Kenny did get better, and his mother was happy with the outcome of him "just playing," although I wondered if she thought that I somehow had "said" something magical to him that she had not been able to say.

Perhaps the real magic is to be found in her admonishment to Kenny about not "just playing." Although she summarized well the sentiment of disregard for the importance of play in our society,

Kenny's mom also pointed to the very element that makes play work so well when we are struggling with difficult problems: It takes us to our growing edge. Play that occurs in a safe and supportive interpersonal environment allows us to temporarily suspend reality enough that we are better able to look at our life situations in a new way. Playing in the presence of another—partly by directly involving the body and partly because of the support provided—allows issues that are often out of sight, in our right hemispheres (stored as emotions, bodily feelings, patterns of action, and perceptions), to bubble to the surface, where we can experience them directly enough to arrange and rearrange them playfully in different patterns. It is "just play," after all, and that, coupled with the caring eyes of another, gives us the safety and the courage we need to look at the painful issues, in the symbolic language of play, and to dare to experience them in different ways. Playing within relationship creates safety automatically, for the most part, and safety is the first requirement for therapeutic change or for any long-lasting learning to occur. As Fred Rogers said, "Play allows us a safe distance as we work on what's close to our hearts" (1994, p. 59).

In the past decade, there has been a significant shift in the mental health field toward including a neuroscience perspective when designing clinical interventions. However, for many play therapists, it has been challenging to apply this information in the context of play therapy because of the bias against the importance of play. For school counselors it has been nearly impossible to justify play in the school setting, even with this growing body of information, given the overall climate of pressure to achieve academically at all costs, even if it means eliminating playgrounds, recess, and anything that does not teach children how to take tests that have now become the standard of success at the end of each school year. Although the flow of information from the burgeoning field of neuroscience has been rapid over the past 20 years, there is still insufficient attention placed on how play circuitry can be recruited to create *real therapeutic change* and *long-lasting motivation to learn*, as well as develop the very circuitry that allows children to drink in what is being taught.

We are now at a stage in our understanding when we can develop language to explain the neurobiology of play experiences for those who want to collaborate with the brain's inborn circuitry in educational, healing, or family environments. If we can help parents, teachers, and clinicians understand why play helps children (and adults) heal from painful experiences, while developing self-regulation and empathy, our attempts to collaborate with the playful brain will be met with welcome relief by most. In addition, joy shared in relationship strengthens social bonds, and given that our brains are wired to engage socially from first breath to last, collaborating with the playful brain can only help.

In this book I want to share the words I have found useful in having conversations, not only with parents like Kenny's mom, but also with colleagues, teachers, and even children about the importance of play. I have sought to make these explanations simple and clear, but also based on science. Because of the need to justify our play practices, I have also been dedicated to utilizing neuroscience to find best practices for evidence-based play therapy. As a former teacher, I resonate with the difficulties school counselors, in particular, encounter in justifying their use of play.

Recently, I listened to a young school counselor's story of a third-grade boy who was using puppet play to show her how lonely and isolated he felt when his parents punished him repeatedly with hours of time out in his bedroom. When the classroom teacher found out that the child was playing in the counselor's office, she admonished the counselor for allowing the child to play at school. In response to the teacher's criticism, the counselor switched the child from puppet play to journal writing. Unfortunately, the child's experiential story was lost, and the chance to intervene vanished. The counselor knew in her heart what the child needed, but she could not explain to the teacher the "why" of puppet play. This third grader could use puppet play, an interpersonally connected activity centered in the right hemisphere, to *show* the counselor the problems that were interfering with his ability to focus academically, but he could not *describe* the issue in words perhaps because he felt too much shame and perhaps because the words of the left hemisphere were not connected to his felt sense of his discomfort. Intuitively, the counselor was collaborating with the way the child's mind worked, but she did not have the framework for explaining to the teacher the interpersonal neurobiology that was evident at so many levels.

In this book I am hoping to show you how collaborating with the playful brains of our children, our peers, and ourselves, based on what we know from interpersonal neurobiology, helps us live more joyful and more integrated lives. I have organized the book in three parts. Part I lays a conceptual foundation for considering play in relation to the neurobiology of the developing brain and mind. In Part II we explore a number of topics about play, keeping the brain in mind. We begin with the therapeutic playroom where warm relationships can release the power of play. We then look at what interpersonal neurobiology teaches us about relational play and how it helps to build children's regulatory and empathic circuitry, along with storytelling play as an integrative tool, and the importance of mindfulness as a foundation for connection.

In Part III we consider the state of play in our families, our clinics, and our schools. We ask questions about the diminishment of play over time in our culture. How did we get to this place? And knowing now from a scientific perspective how important play is to our well-being across the lifespan, what can we do to welcome it back into our lives and relationships once again?

Drawing from concepts of interpersonal neurobiology (Badenoch, 2008; Schore, 2009; Siegel, 1999, 2007, 2010, 2012) throughout this book, the benefits of viewing play interventions from the perspective of the power of attunement, neural integration, healthy attachment, and the development of resilience and well-being become clear. This view reflects a current shift in the field of mental health from a medical model of defectiveness and prescription to a focus on how clinicians can collaborate with the natural tendency of all humans to attach to one another, an activity that supports the brain's inherent movement toward integration of its various regions into a coordinated "dance" that supports a life of relational goodness and meaning. In addition, I present a number of clinical cases to illustrate how relational play promotes neural integration. Each case example is based on composite material drawn from numerous clinical experiences. I have done it this way to protect confidentiality of actual patients while preserving the authenticity of the illustrations.

Our exploration of play begins with the story of 6-year-old Alice, who played vigorously with puppets to show me the trauma of the dental surgery she had experienced just before her third birthday. I learned from the intensity of her play just how powerful the mind is in its natural push toward wholeness and integration.

PART I

Concepts of Play

Chapter 1

CREATING SAFETY AND CONNECTION FOR PLAY

Alice handed me two puppets, a wolf and a dolphin, as soon as we got to the playroom. She got the doctor's kit off the shelf and seemed eager to play. I could see from the look in her eye that this was what we were going to do today. It was not the first time we had played with these particular puppets, but it was the first time she had showed any interest in the medical kit. I put the wolf puppet on my left hand and the dolphin on my right. Alice immediately began stuffing the wolf's mouth full of medical instruments from the doctor's play kit. She then taped his jaws tightly shut with a Velcro strap. As the wolf ("Wolfie"), I could easily imagine how overwhelmed and helpless he must have felt. I moved my dolphin puppet ("Dory") close to Wolfie's face and said, "Oh, Wolfie! You can't talk with all that stuff in your mouth." Wolfie whimpered and moaned, tilting his head slightly. "Maybe I can help you," continued Dory, but Wolfie began jumping up and down on the floor, making loud angry sounds. Alice smiled. Dory Dolphin tried to empathize with Wolfie to help him calm down. Alice laughed out loud, and said to me, "Do it again!" I complied, making Wolfie jump up and down somewhat more dramatically while making a variety of angry and distressed sounds.

I let Wolfie rest a moment while Dory moved in to say, "You are really angry, Wolfie!" With mounting excitement, Alice commanded me to do the sequence once again. This time Wolfie hopped around in a circle making loud protesting noises and then fell over on his side. Dory came close to Wolfie, "Here, let me help you," she said. She took the Velcro strap off his jaws, and Wolfie vigorously spit out the medical instruments. Gasping, he turned to her and whispered, "Thank you, Dory, thank you."

During this entire puppet drama, Alice looked at me repeatedly to make sure I was really just playing. She smiled again, and then put the alligator puppet (with zippered jaw) on her right hand, and with her left, she unzipped and then zipped his jaw shut several times. Alice looked up at me, and Dory Dolphin said, "Wolfie, look! I think we may have a new friend." To the alligator, she said, "Hi. What's your name?"

Alice's parents had brought her to me for play therapy several months earlier because of their concern about her academic development. Alice was 6 years old, and she was refusing to speak at school. She did say a few words to her mother during the first two play therapy sessions, but she did not speak directly to me. She avoided eye contact with me and stayed as close as possible to her mother.

At first, when I spoke to Alice, I could see her body stiffen and her face go flat. I knew that I needed to be gentle and that it would be important to proceed slowly. Alice really liked the playroom, however, and I believe she felt safe with me because I soon saw the physical cues that she was relaxing and beginning to interact with me. Even when her mother was not in the playroom, she began to move more freely in the space. By the third session, she was speaking in brief phrases to me, also making eye contact several times.

At the beginning of our work, Alice thoroughly explored all the options in the playroom. She was first attracted to the sand tray and played out numerous sequences that seemed to fit with my initial impression of trauma. She then explored the clay and art materials. When she discovered the puppets, she seemed unsure about how to play with them. I gently introduced her to the idea of the puppets being curious about each other. By this time, Alice was talking more in the playroom (although she was still not speaking at school), and the idea of having the puppets speak for her seemed to appeal to her. Now, well into her therapy, this puppet play with the wolf, the dolphin, and the zippered alligator was giving voice to some aspect of her story.

When I first interviewed the parents to gather history before meeting Alice, I asked them numerous routine questions, including some about medical interventions. Had she ever been to the emergency room? Was there any history of invasive medical procedures? The parents told me that she had needed dental surgery just before her third birthday. I asked them how she had responded to the surgery. The father told me that Alice definitely did not like going to the dentist, even now, but he thought that the outcome of the surgery had been successful, and since Alice had received anesthesia during the procedure, he did not think it had impacted her too much.

Alice's puppet play told a different story, however, and in a follow-up telephone call to her father, I asked for more details of the dental surgery. He said that they had taken Alice to a dentist who specialized in working with children, but they were taken aback by his brusque treatment approach. Alice was quite overwhelmed by the dentist, and her mother had to restrain her in the dental chair to enable him to proceed with his examination. Her father also told me that the surgery had taken much longer than expected, due to some internal problems in the operating room, and that he had been worried about the possibility that Alice might have come out of the anesthesia for periods of time in what must have been a frightening and possibly very painful environment for a 3-year-old with neither parent present.

This more detailed description of the surgery confirmed my diagnosis of posttraumatic stress disorder (PTSD)[1] in conjunction with selective mutism.[2] Coupled with her history of adoption at 10 months of age, Alice's puppet play made sense to me. Alice did not directly identify the play as dental surgery. She spoke no words during the puppet play except to direct me (as the wolf with a mouthful of medical instruments taped shut with a strap) to "do it again" when I paused during my pretend temper tantrums. Alice seemed to be showing me what it was like for a 3-year-old to undergo such a painful and overwhelming trauma. The surgery would have been traumatic enough by itself, but compounding the trauma for Alice was the abandonment she likely experienced in the operating room. In addition, the coldness and lack of relatedness of the dentist surely made her experience a lot worse.

What made it possible for Alice to show me this trauma through the puppet play? How could she enact this sequence without becoming retraumatized? Why did she need to play it out in the playroom with me? Most important, did it decrease her anxiety, and did it help her with her ability to speak at school? Finally, how could I help her parents and teachers understand Alice's play?

EXPLAINING PLAY TO PARENTS AND TEACHERS

It is clear to me that most parents are eager to do everything they possibly can to help their children develop well. It is not always so clear to them that play is an essential ingredient in this development. Because I know that parents need to maximize their time and financial resources when they bring their children to therapy, I include neuroscience explanations about play in the initial interview. I explain how play works in the nervous system, and I use handouts to help them visualize it. I have also found these handouts useful for teachers to show them how play enhances learning through the development of social skills and self-regulation. Often when I am explaining to these adults how play (or lack of play) affects the development of the nervous system, they suddenly recognize their own feelings and behaviors. They get it, not only for their children but also for their own self-awareness. Teachers begin to find ways to incorporate play in their classrooms to enrich and strengthen academic tasks. What follows is a review of some of the concepts from interpersonal neurobiology, including the handouts I use, that seem particularly relevant to play (see the Appendix for handouts you may copy).

Our review begins with the work of two neuroscientists who have directly addressed the topic of play in their scientific studies. We begin with the animal laboratory work of affective neuroscientist Jaak Panksepp (1998, 2005, 2007, 2009; Panksepp & Biven, 2012) and then turn to the polyvagal theory of Stephen Porges (2011; Porges & Carter, 2010) to see if we can weave together their neuroscience concepts of play to help us understand why we need to care about play. What they have to say may help us explain just how fundamental play should be in our society, whether we are in a school classroom, a play therapy clinic, or at home with our children.

THE PUZZLE OF PLAY

It is not easy coming up with a definition of play. Scholars of this subject have argued about what play really is, and most neuroscientists have stayed away from researching play because it is so hard to define with precision—and it is difficult to operationalize for research observation and measurement. Because it is rooted in processes that lie deep within the brain, rather than in the more familiar neocortical/cognitive areas, it defies easy capture and quantification by our conceptual approaches.

Despite these difficulties, neuroscientist Jaak Panksepp (1998, 2009; Panksepp & Biven, 2012) believes so deeply in the value of play that he has devoted his professional life to studying it. Through his laboratory research, he identified specific circuitry for PLAY and at least six other *emotional systems* (also referred to as *motivational* or *affective systems*) in the brain: SEEKING, RAGE, LUST (which manifests at the onset of puberty), FEAR, PANIC/GRIEF/Separation Distress, and CARE (see Figure 1.1) (*Note*: In keeping with Panksepp's presentation of the seven motivational circuits in the brain, we are using capitals to remind us that we are talking about one of the specific core circuits he identified as being intrinsic to all mammals, not just humans.). As we will see, SEEKING is the primary emotional–motivational circuit impacting all of the other circuits. It is active when CARE, LUST, or PLAY emerge in conditions of safety and connection (right side of figure), and it also is active when FEAR and PANIC/GRIEF/Separation Distress emanate from the felt sense of being unsafe and disconnected from sources of support (left side of figure). When SEEKING is thwarted, RAGE arises (also on the left side of figure because this circuit is aroused under conditions of disconnection).

Although society, in general, often regards playing as a waste of time, or at best an unimportant use of time, most children will occupy themselves with play, especially play with others, if they are not required to be involved in more structured tasks. Perhaps this devotion to play that we see in children speaks to the deep inherent need we humans have to play. There are activities we learn, such as reading, that don't spring from an intrinsic motivational system within us. However, a number of activities/actions, such as playing,

MOTIVATIONAL* CIRCUITS IN THE BRAIN
Jaak Panksepp

ACTIVATED WHEN WE ARE **OUT OF CONNECTION** WITH SIGNIFICANT OTHERS	ACTIVATED WHEN WE ARE **IN CONNECTION** WITH SIGNIFICANT OTHERS
• RAGE (anger) • FEAR (anxiety) • PANIC/GRIEF (Separation Distress)	• CARE (nurturance) • LUST (sexual excitement) • PLAY (social joy)
• SEEKING (expectancy)	

*Panksepp sometimes uses the terms, *Emotional Systems* or *Affective Systems* to refer to these seven unique *Motivational Circuits.*

FIGURE 1.1. Panksepp's Seven Motivational Circuits. This arrangement emphasizes the importance of connectedness or disconnectedness in the activation of these key circuits. See Panksepp (1998) for his original discussion.

caring for others, and avoiding fearful situations, are part of our genetic inheritance. Panksepp (2009) calls them "ancestral tools for living" (p. 4).

Although play circuitry has received less attention from neuroscientists than other neural systems, Panksepp underscores its importance as a source of social connection, a way to learn the relational "rules of the road," the ground for expanding knowledge, and "perhaps one of the major brain sources of joy" (Panksepp, 1998, p. 281). Through his animal laboratory studies, Panksepp has provided data establishing the existence of play circuitry in the brains of all mammals (a category that includes us humans). Although most of the recent research on play has taken place with animals only, Panksepp also cites research studies from the era of psychosurgery providing scientific evidence for these same systems in humans (Heath, 1996; Panksepp, 1985).

What is play? According to Panksepp (2009), "There is a jester in all of us. Thank goodness, for it can make play out of work—including, potentially, psychotherapeutic work" (p. 16). He goes on to suggest, "It is a blessing that the urge for social play—for joyous physical engagement with others—was not left to chance by evolution, but is built into the instinctual action apparatus of the mammalian brain" (p. 16). In other words, it is a core, genetically established system that simply has to be engaged, not something that has to be built from experience—although it is also true that experience shapes how we engage (or don't engage) in play. He further highlights the social nature of these joyous activities:

> Playfulness is probably an experience-expectant process that brings young animals to the perimeter of their social knowledge, to psychic places where they must learn about what they can or cannot do to each other. Play allows animals to be woven into their social structures in effective but friendly ways. . . . Young animals readily communicate how much they enjoy these activities, partly by play vocalizations (e.g., 50 kHz chirps in rats) that can also be induced by tickling them. (2009, pp. 16–17)

These vocalizations amount to rodent laughter, not dissimilar from the joyous sounds emanating from Alice as she and I played with Wolfie, Dory, and the zippered alligator. Her ability to engage with me in this raucous exchange was built on the foundation of safety we had created in our play space. Most mammals do not play when frightened or when they detect danger, since their core security then shifts to efforts to ensure survival. Hunger and illness, conditions in which safety can also feel compromised, also diminish play or even eliminate it.

The capacity for play appears to emerge early in infancy and usually in the safety of parent–child social bonds, especially between mothers and infants. Here, we can see it situated with its companion systems, CARE and SEEKING. With warm attention and curiosity, mother and baby explore the ascending scale of laughter and delight, and in ideal conditions, mothers can sense when their young ones have had enough, helping them calm down again. This kind of interchange builds the regulatory circuitry, gradually helping children develop the capacity for rich and well-regulated emotional experience throughout their lives. According to research, the most vigorous play occurs in the context of preexisting social bonds (Panksepp, 1998; Siviy, 2010)—a finding that makes sense in light of the connection between bonding and play. (We will talk more about play and attachment in Chapters 3 and 5).

Because in this book we are interested in interpersonal play, we will focus our discussion on relational play—that is, interactive play in educational, home, and therapeutic environments. Fred Rogers captures the essence of why it is so difficult to define play: "It is not easy to come up with a definition of play that feels just right. And that's probably because something deep within all of us 'knows' the immense value of play" (Rogers, 1994, p. 63). Panksepp's research has gone a long way toward helping us understand the "deep within" nature of the play circuitry and its power to bring us peels of laughter in the midst of social connection.

Surely Alice understood "the immense value of play" deep inside her, beneath any verbal awareness. She used the puppet play spontaneously to access a deeply painful and frightening experience. Through our mutual play, she was able to bring her trauma forward into the play therapy room, where what she was experiencing was held between us. In that safe context, her brain had a chance, in conjunction with the safety she experienced with me, to rewire the neural pathways that were limiting her capacity for social engagement through language in specific situations. I wanted to help her parents understand just how hard Alice was working on her traumatic experiences as we played so vigorously and with such delight.

PLAY CIRCUITRY IN THE BRAIN AND THE NERVOUS SYSTEM

How did Alice access her traumatic experiences when we played together without getting overwhelmed? In this section we are going to review briefly how the nervous system works in the context of play. We will explore the bi-directional nature of the nervous system and the embodied brain to help us see how play helps to develop self-regulation as we move into the polyvagal theory proposed by

Stephen Porges (2011). He offers us a *traffic signal* analogy to assist us in understanding this important scientific discovery in the context of play.

Reviewing the Nervous System

Here we turn to the work of Stephen Porges, a pioneering researcher who has illuminated the nature of the autonomic nervous system, and particularly its role in interpersonal experiences such as play. To help us get oriented, let's look more closely at the brain in the context of the nervous system so that we can better understand the importance of safe conditions in encouraging play, and also get an idea about how interactive play helps us develop self-regulation.

Technically, if we consider what current neuroscience is telling us, it is more accurate to talk about the *embodied brain* rather than to picture it as existing only in the skull. We are learning that brain functions are distributed throughout our bodies (Badenoch, 2011; Siegel, 2010) and that the heart and the entire digestive tract have extensive networks of nerves that allow them to process complex information as they relay data upward to, and receive data downward from, the part of the brain in the skull. Badenoch (2011) talks about a "heart brain" and a "gut brain" in addition to the brain in the skull. Siegel (2010) describes how nerve cells are dispersed throughout the body during early development in the womb and how the spinal cord forms when the cells that form the outer layer of the embryo fold inward. He talks about how clusters of wandering cells then start to gather at one end of the spinal cord to become what we think of as the skull-encased brain. Other neuronal tissue becomes interwoven with our musculature, our skin, heart, lungs, and digestive system. This concept of the embodied brain will help us understand how play facilitates the development of self-regulation.

In Figure 1.2, we can see the bidirectional nature of the nervous system, which brings the outer world in through our sensory nerves at the periphery to our spine and then up to our skull-encased brain. And in reverse, we can see how energy and information also flow from the skull-brain to the periphery.

The central nervous system (CNS) is comprised of the skull brain and the spinal cord. The peripheral nervous system divides into the

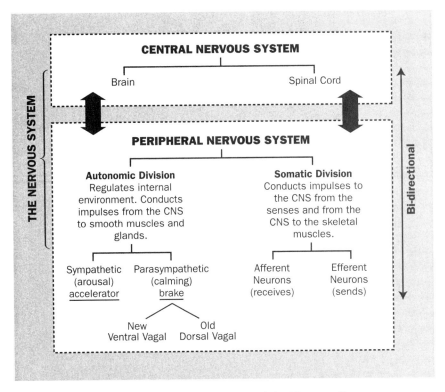

FIGURE 1.2. A Schematic Representation of the Nervous System to Illustrate Its Bidirectional Functioning.

autonomic and the somatic nervous systems. The autonomic nervous system (ANS) includes the sympathetic nervous system (SNS) and the parasympathetic nervous systems (PNS). The SNS acts as an accelerator or an arousal system, whereas the two branches (old and new) of the PNS have a braking function that can either prepare the system for connecting with others (ventral vagal parasympathetic) or lead to diminished consciousness (dorsal vagal parasympathetic). In the somatic nervous system, impulses are sent (efferent) to and received (afferent) from the CNS, mediating physiological and psychological changes.

Using the diagram of the nervous system in Figure 1.2 and keeping the picture of the embodied brain in mind, let's turn to the ideas of Stephen Porges, who uses his polyvagal theory to discuss how play functions in the nervous system.

The Polyvagal Theory: The Traffic Signal Analogy

Porges (Porges & Carter, 2010) sometimes uses a traffic signal analogy to introduce the three branches of the ANS in his polyvagal theory (Figure 1.3). A green light, so to speak, from our nervous system signals that we are safe; a yellow light signals danger; and a red light warns us that we are sensing a life-threatening situation. Porges says that we can encourage people to celebrate the adaptive functioning of the ANS because of how rapidly this system can shift from one physiological state to another in the service of protecting us. He coined the word *neuroception*[3] to describe how we are geneti-

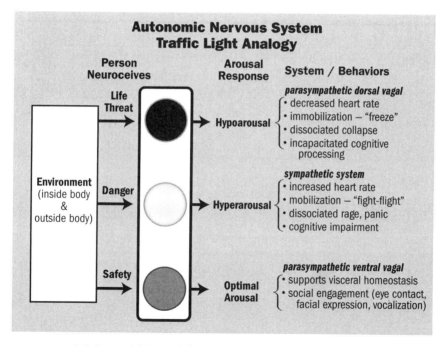

FIGURE 1.3. Porges's View of the Autonomic Nervous System: Traffic Light Analogy. Adapted from Porges (2011, 2012; Porges & Carter, 2010). Used by permission of Stephen Porges.

13

cally wired to detect safety, danger, or threat, even below the level of conscious awareness, when we are challenged (internally or externally) by the environment. This neural surveillance system, organized in a hierarchy, works without our conscious awareness, and it helps us to manage our biobehavioral quest to maintain safety in connection with others.

According to Porges's theory, three evolutionarily based circuits—parasympathetic dorsal vagus, sympathetic system (i.e., SNS), and parasympathetic ventral vagus—operate automatically in our bodies to help us adapt to various conditions in our environments. In contrast to prevailing theories of maintaining a balance between sympathetic and parasympathetic circuits, Porges says we need to account for a third circuit, which he calls the "old" dorsal vagal circuit, to explain how the ANS works. In addition, he says that the three different circuits come "online" in a hierarchical manner, in *reverse* of the order in which they developed during our evolution.

When we have a neuroception of safety (a green light), we automatically use what Porges terms our *social engagement system*, or as he also calls it, the "smart" ventral vagal parasympathetic system. It is the speedy myelinated[4] branch of the 10th cranial nerve, and it gives us access to all the parts of our social engagement system to stay in connection with others. When this circuit is active, we experience optimal levels of arousal in our nervous system, and we are able to pay attention well by efficiently accessing our cerebral cortex. We use eye contact, facial expressions, and head turning to communicate with other humans.

We also can modulate our feelings and express ourselves through vocalizations that convey safety (e.g., sounds produced in the middle range of the voice—sounds that are neither too shrill [high pitched] nor too booming [low pitched] let others know that we are feeling safe). Because this branch of the nervous system is entangled with the nerves that control the striated muscles of the face, our animated visage conveys a sense of safety to those approaching us, an invitation to come in and settle down together. Our inner ear muscles modulate in response to the pitch (low to high) of the vocal sounds produced by others so that we are able to listen for the qualities of safety in others. For example, Porges (2011) notes, "The lower pitch associated with a booming voice will often startle and/or frighten the observer, while the high pitch of a shrill voice will generally evoke

anxiety and fear" (p. 249). This myelinated branch of the vagus also connects the brain stem and the heart, with the latter connection allowing for the application of the vagal "brake" that quiets our heart rate, one of the subtle signals that we are experiencing safety. This vagal "setting" is the preferred mode of operation in the nervous system—a preference that makes sense since we are hardwired from before birth to our last breath to connect with others. In this way, the nervous system is designed to support secure attachments with our parents. In this safe physiological state we have maximum access to our cognitive resources.

If, however, our nervous system detects that we may be in danger (yellow light), our social engagement system will go offline and the SNS will become active. We will move into a cautionary or protective mode, automatically mobilizing defensive strategies of fight or flight. If we can protect ourselves by fighting, we will, but if fighting does not seem viable, we will try to flee. These behaviors dampen our cognitive functioning, narrowing the amount of new information we take in so that we can focus exclusively on the source of the threat. We may become hypervigilant as we begin to engage subcortical areas of the brain more actively in order to respond swiftly to the danger. Our heart rate increases (release of the vagal brake) as we experience the rapid engagement of our whole system to ensure our survival. With decreasing capacity to take in new information and our social engagement system offline, it will be difficult for us to regulate ourselves, or for others to regulate us, until our sense of safety is restored. Although we may not have full access to our cognitive or interpersonal resources, our nervous system is functioning well as it switches efficiently into this more protective mode.

In a situation our system senses to be life-threatening, often because we have a neuroception of helplessness and fighting or fleeing can no longer protect us, a danger signal (red light) comes on, activating the third branch of the ANS, the dorsal vagal parasympathetic (the slower, unmyelinated branch). Our nervous system goes into a *freeze mode* as we try to defend ourselves by feigning death or shutting down (reduced heart rate, cessation of digestion, collapse, dissociation). We may feel numb and become passive with decreased sensations. At this point, our cognitive processing is severely impaired or goes offline completely as our physiological system takes over to protect us from painful experiences through a release of endorphins.

Because of this impairment, wherein we become immobilized or freeze in a reptilian state, conserving bodily resources, Porges (2011) calls this branch the "old" dorsal vagal system. In this energy-conserving state, it is difficult, if not impossible, for the highly oxygen-dependent cortex to operate.

We can see that the nervous system "prefers" its most recently developed social engagement mode, falling back on the earlier mammalian mode only when the social engagement system fails. If the mammalian system fails, it then falls back on the reptilian mode. This reversed functioning of the nervous system, in terms of its evolutionary development, reflects quite a different process from that envisioned by the old balance theories of sympathetic and parasympathetic functioning. Porges's vagal theory has highly salient implications for parenting, clinical practice, and educational strategies. Part III details how we can assess, in real time, various modes of the nervous system and what the implications are for helping our children, patients, and students reconnect with their "smart" (and preferred) ventral vagal tendencies. Porges's theory also has numerous implications for play behaviors and play therapy, which we will also explore.

The Green Light of Play

For 3-year-old Alice, dental surgery could easily have seemed like a life-threatening situation, causing her body, particularly her mouth and facial muscles, to shut down. Alice's response made sense in the dental chair and in the operating room, but 3 years later it was not serving her well, and the challenge for her parents, her teacher, and then for me as her therapist was how to help her restore her social engagement system so that she could relax and begin to speak at school.

Paradoxically, when our nervous system detects danger and we have a fight–flight–freeze response, the memory of the traumatic experience is seared into bodily based implicit memory while it may be simultaneously blocked from explicit memory. We know that explicit memory develops gradually, from the second year of life until the circuitry is complete at about 5 years of age, so it seemed likely that Alice would have mainly implicit memories of her dental experience even without the trauma. We will talk more about implicit and explicit memories in Chapter 5.

When Alice played out her trauma with the puppets, she was accessing implicit memories (emotions, bodily sensations, bodily movements, and perceptions, stored primarily in the right hemisphere) so that she could integrate them into an explicit story of Wolfie, Dory, and the alligator. Although the puppet play did not result in factual memories for Alice, it allowed her to make sense of the bodily sensations that she likely felt during a painful and frightening dental experience.

Why did Alice need to travel this indirect route of playful behavior to make sense of her trauma so that she could shift back into her social engagement system? Does she need to bring the trauma memories to verbal awareness for healing to occur? Porges (2009, 2011) believes that play helps us to mobilize (sympathetic arousal) without losing our ability to stay socially engaged (ventral vagus). In this sense, Alice was using aspects of the SNS in the service of exploring adaptive defensive and aggressive behaviors through "just playing."

We can imagine how Alice would have gone into sympathetic arousal (fight–flight) and then dropped into dorsal vagal (freeze) when her mother had to restrain her in the dental chair while a rather large and overwhelming dentist probed her teeth. Playing with the puppets allowed Alice to reenact the dental experiences in the context of our safe relationship and our full engagement with one another—neither of which was present in the initial experience. When I (as Wolfie) responded to the mouthful of medical instruments that Alice had taped shut with a Velcro strap, I was pretending to mobilize to fight–flee. In the safe context of our play, Alice was delighted with Wolfie's temper tantrum and his effort to run away when Wolfie's SNS came online. As she commanded me to repeat Wolfie's tantrum, it must have been a great relief for her to experience the sympathetic arousal of the wolf puppet while simultaneously controlling the wolf's behavior. As Wolfie fell over, she may also have been able to experience the dorsal vagal collapse that may have occurred because of the helplessness, either in the dental chair or on the operating table.

At another level, she was looking at me, checking to see if my facial expression was conveying safety, to make sure that we were "just playing." The "just playing" physiological state allowed us both to stay in our social engagement systems (new ventral vagus), to stay connected with one another, as we reworked the experiences of the sympathetic arousal and the shutdown, or freeze, of the old dorsal vagal system. We were literally holding the terrifying experiences in the embrace of our relationship, facilitated by my steady engagement of the ventral vagal parasympathetic. Our staying connected during the experience allowed the trauma to integrate into Alice's overall brain structure, rather than remaining as a frightening isolated event that was keeping her from being able to move toward others.

Not long after the puppet play with the doctor's kit, Alice's parents reported that she began to call out to friends at school when they were on the playground. She even ventured to say good-bye to her teacher when she saw him in the parking lot one day after school. Prior to the puppet play and the subsequent short vocalization bursts at school, I noticed that Alice's body movements were gradually becoming freer during the course of therapy. She began skipping down the walkway to the playroom, waving her arms, rather than following shyly behind her mother, partially hiding as she had done at the beginning.

Keeping Alice's life story in mind along with her use of play activities for healing trauma, in the next chapter we turn our attention to the relational aspects of play circuitry in the brain and nervous system. As we do, so many questions come to mind. Just how early in our development does this ability to play with another appear? When do Panksepp's motivational systems come online? At what stage can we begin to explore play as a way to regulate our nervous systems? As we will see, the answers may be surprising.

CHAPTER NOTES

1. *Post traumatic stress disorder*: a severe anxiety disorder that can develop after exposure to an event that results in psychological trauma.

2. *Selective mutism*: a psychiatric disorder in which a person who is normally capable of speech is unable or unwilling to speak in given situations or to specific people.

3. *Neuroception*: the detection of features in others or the environment—without awareness—that dampens defensive systems and facilitates social behaviors *or* promotes defensive strategies of mobilization

(fight–flight) or immobilization (shutdown, dissociation) (Porges & Carter, 2010).

4. *Myelination*: a myelin layer (or sheath) around the axon of a neuron. It increases the speed at which impulses propogate along the *myelinated* fiber.

Chapter 2

EARLY PLAY EXPERIENCES

When Maria, the governess in the *Sound of Music,* tries to teach the children how to sing by explaining musical notes, she realizes they don't get it, and she simply begins to sing that wonderful song about starting at the very beginning. She tells them that this is the very best place to start, and then she compares the ABCs of reading with the Do–Re–Mi's of singing. When Maria entered into the music itself and began singing, the children got it immediately, and they quickly joined in. With play, it seems we should do the same. Let's enter play right where it begins. If we do that, we will find ourselves looking at the small units of interactive play relationships, going all the way back to infancy, to the context of trusting family relationships.

By observing infants and their caretakers in the first 6 months of life, we can actually get to the ABCs of play from a brain perspective, by looking at the micro elements of play. We can see how crucial these elements are in the development of secure attachment and in our abilities to gradually develop our capacity for self-regulation. Daniel Stern (1977/2002), a psychiatrist who is one of the pioneers of infant mental health, draws from his early research to talk about the crucial nature of play in becoming a social human being.

We have watched social interactions between caregivers and infants in their homes, in the laboratory, on playgrounds, in parks, on subways, anywhere. The purpose of this search has been to understand how, in the short span of the first six months of life, the infant emerges as a social human being. Somehow, in this brief period that I shall call the first phase of learning about things human, the baby will have learned how to invite his mother to play and then initiate an interaction with her; he will have become expert at maintaining and modulating the flow of a social exchange; he will have acquired the signals to terminate or avoid an interpersonal encounter, or just place it temporarily in a "holding pattern." In general, he will have mastered most of the basic signals and conventions so that he can perform the "moves" and run off patterned sequences in step with those of his mother, resulting in the dances that we recognize as social interactions. This biologically designed choreography will serve as a prototype for all of his later interpersonal exchanges. (Stern, 1977/2002, p. 16)

INFANT–PARENT PLAY: NONVERBAL PROTOTYPE FOR HUMAN COMMUNICATION

In the first 6 months of life, we learn the turn taking, the rhythmic intervals, the tempo, the nonverbal messages, and all the improvisational moves that are required for human communication. All of this before language! In fact, our first experiences of play occur before we can physically navigate, manipulate objects, or say even one word. Play in these early months is limited to purely social interactions—sounds, minimal physical movements, facial expressions, looking at or away from each other, gestures, eye gazing, and shared physical excitement.

This social play, sometimes called *free play* or *unstructured play*, is crucial in the infant's development of the schemas and representations that are required for object constancy—that internal composite picture of mother, father, caretaker, or whomever is in close consistent contact. In this free improvisational play, the infant learns to initiate, maintain, terminate, and avoid interactions with his or her human companions. The child regulates and is regulated by the play interactions.

Let's look closely at some of the old tried-and-true games that mothers, fathers, and aunties play with their infants. "Peek-a-boo" and "I'm gonna getcha" are favorites. Having observed the games in the United States, Western Europe, Scandinavia, Eastern Europe, and Russia, Stern (1977/2002) says that they represent some of the most popular of all internationally played baby games. The play begins with adult and baby catching each other's eye, and in the mutual gazing, they signal to one another that they are ready to play. Either partner might initiate a bout of play.

Recently I observed 5-month-old Sammy engage his father in peek-a-boo play. He looked at his dad, and when dad responded by widening his eyes, raising his brows, and looking surprised, Sammy broke into a big smile while simultaneously raising his hands to partially cover his eyes, still peeking through his fingers at his dad. Dad responded by grabbing a kitchen towel to cover his entire head, saying, "Where's Sammy? I can't see him." (*slight pause*). Then dad yanked the towel off his head with a surprised, "There he is!" Sammy giggled. Dad repeated the sequence, only this time he left the towel on his head slightly longer, repeating, but adding a few extra words, "Where's Sammy? I can't see him. (*slight pause*) Where did he go?" Again yanking the towel off his head, he raised his voice slightly and repeated his earlier phrase, "There he is!" This time Sammy broke into full-bodied laughter.

As his laughter faded, Dad looked at Sammy and waited for his son to signal that he wanted more play. Sammy partially covered his eyes again. Dad said, "Oh, you like this game, huh? OK, here goes!" Dad escalated the play by covering his head with the towel, lowering his voice, repeating the earlier question, "Where's Sammy?" Only this time, he repeated the question three times, with the second and third repetitions slightly more drawn out and suspenseful than the previous, ending with a tone of mounting excitement. The towel came off his head with a loud exclamation of "There he is!" and an emphatic, "I found him!" Dad suddenly reached over and tickled Sammy's belly. Sammy squealed with laughter, but then as his laughter peaked, he turned his head away from Dad with a sober expression on his face. This last raucous surprise from Dad and the belly tickling were a little too stimulating. It put Sammy over the top. Not only had Sammy initiated the play with his father, he also terminated it—at least for the moment. Dad picked Sammy up and snuggled him gently, whispering quietly, "Hey, that was fun." Sammy reestablished eye contact.

PLAY IN THE NERVOUS SYSTEM

Using this peek-a-boo game as an example of how parent and infant co-regulate one another, we can see how play interactions function to help infants with the process, as Stern (1977/2002) says, "of learning about things human" (p. 16). In these social interactions, as the infant nervous system develops, babies learn how to regulate their interactions with all the important people who are in close contact with them. If we make a diagram (Figure 2.1) of the brief play period of Sammy and his father, we can get a good idea of how these play interactions help to establish optimal ranges of play behaviors, allowing stimulation and joy to be balanced with rest and comfort, and of how infants and parents co-regulate the moments of hyper-arousal and hypoarousal that happen during play.

We can see in the diagram that optimal play arousal lies within the two lines that define "too much" or "too little" stimulation. The broken line shows how play sequences use parents' more mature

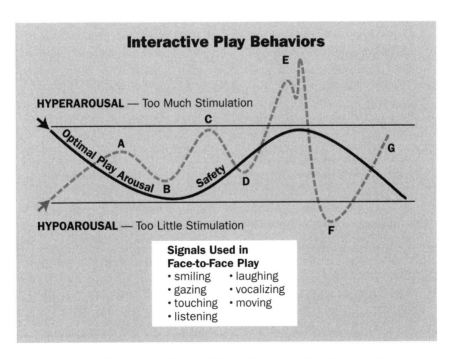

FIGURE 2.1. Tracing the Units of Play Behavior in the Nervous System.

capacities for self-regulation to gradually help their infants develop their own regulatory resources by together testing the limits of what is optimal, and then doing the repairs necessary to come back into an optimal range. After Sammy signaled to his father that he wanted to play, Dad engaged with him by covering his head. When dad yanked the towel off his head, Sammy's nervous system responded with elevated arousal (Point A), but still in the optimal range. As Sammy's arousal decreased (Point B), Dad covered his head again and waited slightly longer, and then using a slightly louder voice, yanked the towel again. Sammy responded with full-bodied laughter (Point C, slightly more arousal than Point B). As Sammy's laughter faded (Point D), Dad waited a moment, and then Sammy signaled that he wanted still more play by partially covering his eyes. Dad escalated the play by lowering his voice and using more repetitions of "Where's Sammy?" He drew each question out slightly longer than the last, and then ended with an emphatic short burst "I found him!" Simultaneously he reached over and tickled Sammy's belly, getting a loud squeal of delight (Point E, overstimulation) from Sammy. As his laughter peaked, Sammy turned his head away from Dad with a sober expression (Point F, withdrawal from stimulation). Dad, accurately reading Sammy's signal, picked him up for a gentle snuggle, and Sammy, returning to the optimal range through this calm, warm interpersonal connection, reestablished eye contact (Point G).

These brief play sequences usually happen spontaneously, intuitively, and naturally for most infant–adult pairs. Most adults use a theme-and-variation approach when engaging in play with infants, as did Sammy's father. The theme (disappearance–reappearance) helps to establish structure, continuity, and a sense of safety, while the variations (timing, loudness or softness of vocalizations, and rhythmical surprises) keep the infant from getting bored, given that babies habituate quickly. We'll talk more about these elements when we discuss the role of play in attachment.

Thankfully, when therapists play with children, they don't have to think about these play strategies or the micro units of play anymore than we have to think about do–re–mi when we sing a song. In our example, the interactive play between Sammy and his father flowed quite naturally. Although it may have looked like the father "messed up" a bit by being a little too stimulating at one point, it is actually important that Sammy have some "over-the-top" and some "under-the-bottom" play experiences. There is virtue in the "messing up" because it gives infants opportunities to explore how to regulate the stimuli coming into their nervous systems, and also to experience and trust parent responses that draw them back into regulated connection.

Sammy self-regulated the hyperarousal by turning his head and looking away from his father. It was equally important that Sammy's father could read the signals of "too much" or "too little" so that he could adjust the amount of stimuli he was providing. In the language of attachment, it is an example of a rupture in the relationship followed by repair. Without these interactive play sequences involving positive affect, it would be difficult for infants to learn how to adapt to the ongoing and often surprising stimuli that they will experience throughout their lives from the environment.

WHY THE MICRO ANALYSIS?

Since all of these play interactions happen quite naturally, why bother with this micro analysis? None of us really needs to know about do–re–mi to sing a song, or ABC to speak a sentence or engage in a conversation. Truthfully, we don't need to know the micro units of play and how they tumble over one another when we are engaged in a playful bout with another human being. On the other hand, getting the feeling of the movement through the stages and understanding the details may help us sense the value of play as "glue" for the secure relationship between parent and infant, as well as gain appreciation for its importance in the infant's development of resources for self-regulation. If we, as therapists, understand the interpersonal neurobiology of play, we may be able to relax about engaging in playful activities in our clinical work. In addition, we may be able to explain to parents, from a brain perspective, why it is so important to make sure their children have ample time for and access to unstructured "free play."

With this knowledge under our belts, we don't have to rely only on general statements in supporting our play activities with children by saying, "It's good for them," or "Play helps them let off steam," or "Play is the language of children." All of these things are true, and it is also true that it is just wonderful to engage in the pure joy of play—just because. The interpersonal neurobiology of play teaches us that play is crucial for developing a nervous system that can respond to the ups and downs of life.

WEAVING TOGETHER PANKSEPP'S PLAY CIRCUITRY AND PORGES'S NEUROCEPTION OF SAFETY

In this section we are revisiting the work of two neuroscientists who have specifically worked with the concept of PLAY as it manifests in the nervous system. Using our examples of Sammy playing with his father and Alice trying to resolve experiences of early abandonment and trauma, we will explore how some of the theoretical and labora-tory research findings of these scientists might apply. How does interactive play support the development of self-regulation in the nervous system? And how do the motivational (emotional/affective) systems intertwine as the nervous system dampens or potentiates them depending on how safe a person feels in a particular environ-ment? We will look specifically at Porges's polyvagal definition of play to give us a clearer idea of how interactive play potentially can help youngsters develop resilient nervous systems.

Primary Motivational–Emotional Circuitry

Returning to our interweaving of Panksepp's seven core motiva-tional systems and Porges's polyvagal theory (see Chapter 1), let's look more closely at how play affects the nervous system to see what happens in the life of a child when interactive play goes well and when it does not. In our example of Sammy, we can see how he and his father co-regulated one another, briefly touching the zones of hyperarousal and hypoarousal as they delighted in one another. They were "just playing," and so it was easy and natural to push the limits, over and under, in the service of having fun. Dad was attuned to Sammy, and Sammy recovered quickly from the hyper- and the hypoarousal of their playful exchanges.

Clearly, the play of Sammy and his father was joyful and effective in terms of nervous system regulation, but what about situations when a parent or caretaker rarely attends and seldom meets the child's intrinsic motivation to play? Let's use the example of Alice again to imagine what might have happened during her infancy. We saw how she used the puppets to access early unresolved trauma when she was just 6 years old (see Chapter 1), but we can also imagine a scenario earlier in her life when play may not have gone so well. From her symptoms and from the little history we have about her life in a foreign country during her first 10 months in an orphanage, we might assume that a lot of things did not go well early on.

Let's imagine Alice in her crib in an understaffed and overcrowded orphanage. The walls are somewhat bare, and the temperature is a little too cool. Food is in short supply. Alice is 3 months old. She is wet and a little hungry. She fusses, but when no one comes immediately, she begins to cry. As time passes, she begins flailing around, kicking and waving her arms. She kicks off her blanket, making things a little worse. As her cries become more frantic, an orphanage worker comes to her crib, one in a long row of small ones, each with a baby less than 2 years of age. The caretaker is busy, so she changes Alice's diaper quickly and tucks her blanket snugly around her. During those few moments, Alice searches the eyes of the caretaker, trying to make contact. The caretaker looks at her, but only fleetingly, not the long gazing typical of securely connected mother–infant pairs. As the caretaker bustles away, Alice is left with painful and frightening feelings of abandonment and another failed attempt to connect—which, when repeated often enough, becomes a felt sense of her worthlessness and an anticipation that no one will stay with her.

Looking again at Panksepp's seven motivational circuits, or core emotions, in the brain (Figure 2.2), we can see how some of these core emotions would have been activated in Alice when she began to fuss. Recall that these motivational circuits are genetically inherited and do not need to be learned; nor are they in any way dependent on experience or cognition. SEEKING is the core emotional–motivational circuit that moves us forward. Panksepp and Biven (2012) call it "a goad without a goal" (p. 96). The other systems help to define that goal. When we are out of connection with others, we are vulnerable from birth to the core emotions of RAGE, FEAR, and PANIC/GRIEF/Separation Distress. In the case of FEAR and PANIC/GRIEF/Separation Distress, SEEKING focuses on relief from the misery of disconnection. RAGE arises when we are thwarted

Panksepp's Building Blocks of the Emotional System

Emotional Primes: Ancestral Tools for Living

Blue-Ribbon Emotions — generate well organized behavior sequences that can be evoked by localized electrical stimulation of the brain.

SEEKING / Desire System: the epicenter of the excitement of living, much of which consists of the pursuit of rewards; the active explorer inside the brain to find resources, to make new discoveries, and to serve as a foundation for practically all the libidinal aspirations of the human heart; a well-being system; a generalized substrate for all the other emotional processes, from establishing libidinal social bonds to seeking safety in dangerous situations.

RAGE / Anger System: the primal source of angry feelings, readily aroused by restraint and frustration, particularly when organisms do not get what they SEEK and want; often intertwined with the FEAR system.

FEAR / Anxiety System: provides a sentry function to alert organisms to all kinds of dangers that threaten the integrity of the body and of life itself; promotes generalized anxiety disorders, neurotic disorders, and specific phobias.

PANIC / GRIEF / Separation Distress System: major source of psychic pain; mediates separation-distress calls (crying); crucial for social attachment; parallels the CARE system.

Special-Purpose Socioemotional Systems — less understood in terms of research data, but engaged by all mammals at appropriate times throughout the life span.

LUST / Sexual Urges: a core sensualist system somewhat differentiated in males and females; not fully activated until puberty; linked with the SEEKING system.

CARE / Nurturance System: maternal love and caretaking, heightened by increased levels of oxytocin and prolactin; intertwined with dopamine.

PLAY System: the emotional system that produces feelings of joy; although motivation for play is located in the subcortex, it is capable of programming the cortex to become truly social; located in brain regions rich in opioids and dopamine.

FIGURE 2.2. Panksepp's "Blue-Ribbon" and "Special-Purpose" Core Emotions (Adapted from Panksepp, 1998, 2009).

and lose hope in finding that solace. In connection, SEEKING allows us to pursue the core emotions of CARE, LUST, and PLAY in all kinds of creative ways.

More than likely, when no one responded to Alice's cries, she felt FEAR—that subcortical circuit that activates when our survival is threatened. The activation of this system would be reflected in her fearful face and sounds as she was employing her SEEKING system to draw someone to her. When she began to flail around, thrusting her arms and legs, she probably experienced RAGE, the feeling we contact when we are unable to move toward something that we're SEEKING. In this case, Alice was trying to activate her caregiver's CARE system to get her physical and emotional needs met. Because the caretaker had so little time to really attend to Alice's emotional needs, we expect that Alice's PANIC/GRIEF/Separation Distress system, the one that promotes attachment, was activated when the interaction was cut short.

For this pair, without connection, there was little chance for the core emotion of CARE, Panksepp's term for maternal love and care-taking, or for the activation of the PLAY system, the emotional system that produces feelings of joy. We also know that Alice's SEEKING system was turned on and then quickly thwarted as she searched the caretaker's eyes for connection. Panksepp says that SEEKING is "the basic impulse to search, investigate and make sense of the environment" (1998, p. 145). Unfortunately, Alice received little reinforcement for the positive core emotions. She was left to comfort herself or even to dissociate—a state in which the SEEKING system turns off—to protect herself from the unbearable feelings of disconnection. We can probably assume that this interaction is just one example of the numerous times 3-month-old Alice has already received this response to her SEEKING efforts to establish a social connection with her caregivers.

In contrast, 5-month-old Sammy displays well-developed play interactions with his father, and we can assume that he has had many stimulating and satisfying social interactions involving his intertwining motivational systems of SEEKING and PLAY in response to his father's activated CARE system. He probably experienced most of these interactions within his optimal range of tolerance for stimulation. If the stimulation exceeded or fell short of the optimal range, more than likely one of his parents quickly attuned to him, helping him to regulate his nervous system. We can see from this example that the PLAY system is often embedded in, and arises from, activities springing from the CARE and SEEKING systems in this relational pair.

Looking at the micro details of Sammy playing with his father and Alice crying out for attention from her caretaker, we can see six of Panksepp's seven emotional primes coming into play (Figure 2.2). We did not see the LUST system since it is one of Panksepp's "special-purpose" systems that, like CARE and PLAY, activates only at appropriate times throughout life. Panksepp says that these emotional primes are the building blocks of our fundamental life experiences. They are the primary tools we use as we adapt to the challenges we face from our environment.

A NERVOUS SYSTEM THAT DAMPENS OR POTENTIATES CORE EMOTIONS

This coverage of Panksepp's theory in relation to our two infants, Alice and Sammy, brings us back to Stephen Porges's concepts of the neuroception of safety and his traffic light analogy of the nervous system. He points out that Panksepp's seven motivational systems are dampened or potentiated depending on the person's neuroception of safety. In Alice's case, the positive core emotions would have been dampened and the negative ones heightened due to the role that visceral state plays in neural regulation. Porges (2011) explains:

> . . . if an individual is in a physiological state characterized by vagal withdrawal and high sympathetic excitation, body feelings of a fast pounding heartbeat are experienced and the threshold to react aggressively is low. In contrast, when in a physiological state characterized by an engaged myelinated vagus, sympathetic and hypothalamic–pituitary–adrenal axis reactivity are dampened. The physiological state is experienced as "calm." Intrusive stimuli that previously would have triggered aggressive behaviors when the vagal activity is withdrawn will now result in a dampened reaction. Accompanying this change in physiological state are options to further dampen reactivity through social interactions. (p. 260)

Porges believes that neuroscientists have underappreciated the complex interactions that transpire between the sensory inputs from the periphery that influence the central circuits and the motor outputs in the periphery that are driven by the central circuits. He says that focusing on the central circuits without taking into account the sensory and motor contributions from the periphery is like trying to explain the behavior of a thermostat without accounting for the input of ambient temperature or the capacities of the heating, ventilation, and air-conditioning elements on the thermostat.

How would Porges's concepts apply to our example of Alice in the orphanage? Recall that our human preference is to stay in the optimal zone of social engagement (ventral vagal), very much like the optimal range of play behaviors that we saw in Figure 2.1. Using Porges's traffic light analogy, we can see how Alice's ANS was functionally adaptive. Had her caretaker been able to respond quickly with her CARE system when Alice first began to activate her SEEKING system through fussing, Alice would have felt safe (potentiating her PLAY system and dampening her RAGE, FEAR, and PANIC systems). Her needs would have been met through the social engagement system (a familiar face, the sound of a voice she recognized, prolonged gazing, and a soothing touch).

When no one responded, Alice likely experienced the yellow light of danger (sympathetic system). Her nervous system would have moved automatically into hyperarousal with increased heart rate and an urge to mobilize. Although infants cannot fight or run away, we see that she did begin to mobilize by flailing around, waving and thrusting her arms and legs. This stimuli—sensory input from her visera (including increased heart beat) and her motor output (flailing arms and legs)—would have potentiated her RAGE, FEAR, and PANIC systems, making her less available to receiving comfort from the CARE system of the orphanage worker. Nonetheless, when her caretaker arrived, Alice's nervous system calmed enough so that her SEEKING system tried to engage her caretaker's eyes. If her caretaker had been able to return the gaze, it would have helped Alice to reestablish a neuroception of safety. Unfortunately, her need for sustained attention was unmet, and for an infant this would constitute danger amounting to a sense of annihilation. In Alice's case, she no doubt would have experienced the PANIC/GRIEF/Separation Distress Panksepp describes as being so intertwined with the CARE system (crucial for social attachment). Receiving little comfort and then quick abandonment, Alice likely dissociated, descending into a state of life threat—the red light—characterized by helplessness and the extreme hypoarousal associated with decreased heart rate and immobilization.

We will return to our interweaving of Panksepp's play circuitry and Porges's neuroception of safety when we talk about treatment using play therapy in Part III. We will explore these complex interactions of the sensory inputs and motor outputs in the periphery with the central circuits in the brain. Building on the concept of the role of play in developing a resilient nervous system during infancy, we will see how we can best use play to heal when, as in Alice's case, opportunities for attachment were not optimal.

Rearranging the Traffic Light Analogy

Let's see what happens when we combine Porges's traffic light analogy with our sketch of the interactive play behaviors that we considered in Figure 2.1. If we place the optimal arousal zone of Porges's green light of safety analogy in the middle (where we had optimal play arousal), and then put the hyperarousal zone, indicating danger above the optimal zone, and the hypoarousal, indicating life threat below the optimal zone, we have a depiction (Figure 2.3) that is similar to the interactive play behaviors schematically represented in Figure 2.1, where we began.

In this new arrangement, we can still see the hierarchical nature of the nervous system with the social engagement as our number one preference (optimal arousal zone), followed by number two (hyperarousal), the strategy we use if the social engagement system fails, and then number three (hypoarousal) if we "neurocept" a life-threatening situation. In addition, we can see the specific behaviors or symptoms associated with each of the three modes of the nervous system. For example, when Alice's caretaker hurried way, an observer would likely have seen a quieter baby (reduced physical movement), but may not have realized that the stillness represented a life-threatening dissociated collapse. Alice, at only only 3 months of age, probably experienced decreased sensation and emotional numbing.

This hierarchy of arousal zones or "window of tolerance" (Siegel,

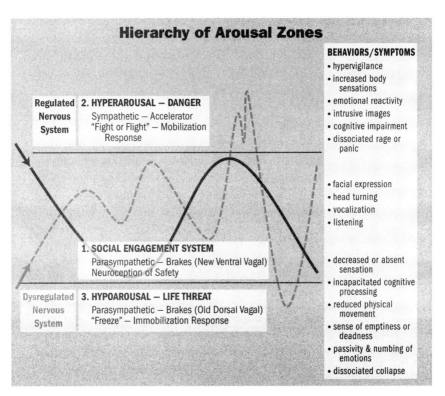

FIGURE 2.3. Hierarchy of Arousal Zones in Porges's Polyvagal Theory. Based on the work of Badenoch (2011), Ogden, Minton, and Pain (2006), Porges (2011), Schore (2009), and Wheatley-Crosbie (2006).

1999) as it is often called in trauma literature (Badenoch, 2008; Ogden et al., 2006; Schore, 2009; Siegel, 2012) helps us to distinguish between a regulated and a dysregulated nervous system. As a reference point, it gives us a way to observe how our patients are functioning in therapy, or how our children are responding to life challenges. In an educational setting, it gives us clear understanding about barriers to learning. We can see that cognitive functioning is impaired, or even absent, when a student, for any reason, leaves the safety of the optimal zone of arousal.

As we will see, like the optimal range of play behaviors, Siegel's (1999) concept of the window of tolerance is a core idea in both the development of self-regulation and in treating trauma. It is also important in establishing a foundation for why play matters, and to understand why the physiological safety of "just playing" is a means for developing a nervous system that can adapt effectively to whatever challenges the environment brings. Equally important, this same physiological safety of "just playing" is a means for healing nervous system trauma.

Remembering our example of Sammy and his father playing peek-a-boo, we can see how important parent–child play is in developing resilience for dealing with strong emotions throughout one's life. While Sammy is expanding his window of tolerance for strong emotions through pairing sympathetic arousal and the pleasure of playing with an important attachment figure, he also is developing his nervous system patterns for coping with the many strong emotions that he will experience throughout life.

The Polyvagal Definition of Play

To understand better how play heals, whether in the family context, a classroom, or a play therapy setting, we can turn to Porges's polyvagal definition of play. He says that play is a blend of the social engagement system (neuroception of safety) *and* the sympathetic system (mobilization of the nervous system in the absence of danger). This blend of these two branches of the nervous system in play arises from the sense of engagement between the players, involving reciprocal face-to-face interactions that are constantly used to assess the intentionality of the actions of others (to make sure that it is "just play" and not aggressive or defensive in some way, as it would be in a fight–flight response generated by a neuroception of danger). Porges (2011) says:

> Thus, play shares with the defensive fight-or-flight behaviors a neurophysiological substrate that functionally increases metabolic output by increasing sympathetic excitation. Current with the sympathetic excitation is a withdrawal of the myelinated vagal pathways that characterize the vagal brake. Just as the primitive mechanisms mediating immobilization in response to life threat can be co-opted to support loving and nutrient processes, so can mobilization mechanisms be involved to facilitate both defensive flight-or-fight behaviors and pleasurable "play." (p. 276)

Although we usually think of mobilization in the nervous system as occurring in the service of aggressive or defensive behaviors, in the case of play, it is different. The face-to-face contact of play gives us a portal through which we can "read" intentionality in others in the striated muscles of their faces, which are entangled with the social engagement branch of the nervous system. Reading the benign intent maintains a neuroception of safety even with heightened arousal.

Following is a summary of the polyvagal definition of play (Porges, 2011, p. 277). It requires:

- Turn taking in expressive motor movements
- Reciprocal receptive inhibition of activity
- Empathy and concern for the well-being of others
- Activation of the sympathetic system (mobilization to support motor activity), followed by a reengagement of the vagal brake of the social engagement system (to restrain mobilization)
- Face-to-face engagement to assess intentionality
- Neuroception of safety that allows rapid recruitment of the social engagement system (to contain potential aggressive or defensive behaviors)

I also have often observed play interactions, such as "playing dead" or "pretending to sleep," that appear to look like the dissociative collapse of the old dorsal vagal system (a reptilian freeze). It may be that play sometimes co-opts the primitive neural mechanisms that mediate immobilization for playful simulation of life-threatening experiences without the reality of the massive reduction of metabolic resources that is involved in dorsal vagal collapse. Porges describes the behaviors involved in nursing, childbirth, and reproductive behaviors as immobilization without fear.

We will return in Part III to Porges's polyvagal definition of play, the hierarchy of arousal zones, optimal play arousal, and Panksepp's core emotions to address the practical implications of these theoretical considerations. As we will see, these concepts are critical in the moment-by-moment treatment decisions that therapists make in clinical environments, and they are also very useful for parents who want to foster adaptive nervous system functioning in their children. *Adaptive nervous system functioning* means better regulated and better behaved children who experience the joy of living and the pleasures of a more harmonious family environment.

Finally, these neuroscience concepts are fundamental for well-functioning educational environments. I strongly believe that our desire for high cognitive functioning in our educational systems will need to take into account Porges's polyvagal theory and Panksepp's core motivational systems. Both of these neuroscientists point to play as an essential element in the core biological functioning of human beings. Play is not just an "extra" gift from Mother Nature.

In the past several decades, mandates have been issued for evidence-based practices in the areas of education and therapy. I believe that our best way forward in meeting these mandates is to collaborate with the fundamentals of how the entire nervous system works, including the skull brain, the embodied brain, the neuroception of safety, and the core emotional systems, including play.

Chapter 3

"WHY CAN'T BOBBY BEHAVE?"

The exasperated tone of the telephone message left by Bobby's father said it all. It left little doubt in the play therapist's mind that things were not going well for her 9-year-old patient. He had recently come to live with his father after being removed from his mother's home by social services in another state. Mr. Andrews was trying hard to make a difference in his son's life, but Dr. Matthews could tell that he was on the verge of giving up. When she returned the father's call that same day, he explained that the school principal had threatened to expel Bobby for violent behavior on the playground. Mr. Andrews said, "I keep telling him to behave. Why can't he listen?"

Dr. Matthews knew that she needed to help Bobby and his father find a way to heal the hurt and trauma resulting from Bobby's early environment of neglect and abuse. She would need to help them develop a trusting relationship that could reach the deep pockets of pain that were driving Bobby's aggressive behavior. By telling him to behave, his dad was speaking clearly to the cortical part of his son's brain, hoping to influence him cognitively and consciously. Bobby's struggle with behavior, however, resided in his early-forming non-verbal subcortical layers, where primary emotional systems, as proposed by Panksepp (see Chapter 2), were strongly influencing his behavior.

To help him change his behavior, Dr. Matthews would need to relate with Bobby in ways that would allow them to co-create new pathways in his brain tying the deep subcortical layers, where Bobby did not feel good about himself and was holding so much pain and fear, together with the cortical layers, so he could gradually gain the circuitry to soothe his raw emotions and regulate his vulnerable nervous system. We can only imagine the countless times he would have experienced the pain and distress of separation when his mother abandoned him, making him no stranger to the feelings of fear and rage that likely would have followed.

Now, at 9 years of age, there were many triggers in his daily experience that rapidly put Bobby in touch with his unregulated core emotional systems. With his father absent and his mother inconsistently available, he had lacked the early intertwining comforts of CARE and the pleasures of PLAY. As a result, his nervous system was highly sensitive to the numerous potential signals of danger and shame in the active environment at school and the increasing upset at home, triggering his overlapping systems of FEAR, RAGE, and PANIC/GRIEF/Separation Distress.

Bobby's stepmother was discouraged as well, and she was finding it more and more difficult to nurture and comfort him as his behavior at home continued to deteriorate. Bobby was having difficulty sensing and respecting her boundaries. Several times he "stole" small objects from her bedroom. He rarely complied with her requests, and after he carved a design in her new coffee table, she realized that she could not turn her back on him for even a moment.

What could be going on in Bobby's brain? Why is he continuously getting into trouble at school and at home? Is something wrong with Bobby? Does he have memory problems? Is he just defective? All of these questions were probably going through his father's mind when he asked, "Why can't he listen?"

The therapist felt confident that Bobby's memory was working well, and she knew that he could behave appropriately. Remarkably, given his history, he was able to cooperate pretty well most of the time. Dr. Matthews liked being with Bobby during his play therapy sessions, and she saw how resilient he was. She was continuously amazed by his creative energy as he moved through various play modalities in her office. She also understood, from an attachment perspective and from having watched Bobby build a number of train wrecks in the sand tray, just why his behavior could fall apart so instantly and unexpectedly in any kind of stressful situation.

Let's rewind in our imaginations to the earliest days of Bobby's life. We find 18-year-old Julie, a first-time mother, struggling to do the right thing with her new infant. She loves Bobby and wants to take good care of him. Julie yearns for him to have a better life than she had growing up. Julie's mother had often been harsh and unpredictable, and her father was seldom at home. He drank too much, had a difficult time holding down a job, and when he was home, he was often emotionally abusive to her mother and physically abusive to her older brother. When Julie was just 6 years old, her father disappeared from the family home, and she never saw him again. This was Julie's first memory of painful abandonment, but it was only the beginning of a series of significant losses, culminating with her husband leaving her when she was 4 months pregnant with Bobby. Julie had few friends and no extended family close by. She tried to work, but her income was barely enough to pay the rent.

Things got even more difficult after Bobby was born and Julie's new boyfriend moved in. Although he had a job and could contribute financially, he was addicted to alcohol and drugs. Julie knew that Bobby needed her, but after stressful days at work, her patience was thin, and it was difficult to comfort him when he cried. It was so easy to begin smoking pot "just a little" with her boyfriend. Soon it was just so easy to close his door and let him cry. Bobby, alone and frightened, learned quickly that he could not always count on his mother to comfort him. He never knew when, or even if, his mother would respond to his cries. Sometimes she came, and sometimes she even played with him, though at times too intensely. He was eager for connection with his mother, but he had no way of predicting when or how he might make that happen.

When we fast-forward to Bobby's current situation (with his biological father and step-mother), we can begin to see how his early life, especially his unpredictable emotional connection with his biological mother, shaped his mind and brain to have certain expectations about how the world would work for him. As a result, at age 9 he had not been able to develop a consistent strategy for dealing with the world. Anticipating abandonment at every turn and accustomed to rage in his household, he was still easily frightened by the angry look of a friend or the slightly raised voice of a teacher. He would feel intensely anxious when a playmate walked away to join others on the playground. His anxiety would turn to fear and rage in a flash, and he was often unable to regulate these deep and intense feelings. Bobby's protective system would act before he could think. Even though he got lots of consequences at home and school, these only served to further sensitize his already vulnerable system. For those around him, it was difficult to understand that he didn't have the neural circuitry to stop the impulse to act.

Hearing Bobby's story, we can get a sense of just how significant his early relationship experiences were. We can begin to appreciate the significance of the question from Bobby's father, "Why can't he listen?" To help Bobby's father begin to understand the forces shaping his son's behavior, Dr. Matthews planned to share what she knew about how implicit memories are formed in the brain, especially within our earliest attachment experiences in infancy and toddlerhood, and how enduring these memories are. She would share her awareness of how these encoded patterns reside in our bodies and guide our actions, also being sure to help him understand that the brain's ongoing capacity to rewire old pathways means that these patterns of attachment and behavior can change within relationships that help Bobby feel safe and understood. She hoped she could foster in Bobby's father new ways of relating with his son that would collaborate with his brain's natural healing processes.

In the remainder of this chapter, we will talk about the organization and integration of the different parts of the brain and mind, creating a foundation for looking at the process of attachment and social bonding in Chapter 5. Each of these topics will be important to Dr. Matthews as she formulates her treatment interventions with Bobby and his father. Pictures of brain and mind have been developed in great depth over the last several decades, creating a starting point for us to address each of these areas, giving special attention to the role of PLAY and the other core emotional systems.

THE LAYERS OF THE DEVELOPING BRAIN

In the last two decades, several perspectives on the way our brain's various structures are related to each other have emerged. They all give a picture of a hierarchical relationship between the structure that developed earliest in evolution (the brain stem), those that developed next and rest on the brain stem (the limbic region, comprised of the amygdala, hippocampus, hypothalamus, and thalamus), and the last to develop, the outer covering that surrounds the limbic midbrain (the neocortex). All point to how the earlier developing regions are embedded in and continually inform the later ones. With the advent of the field of interpersonal neurobiology, we are coming to appreciate even more the nature of this hierarchy and how it develops within our earliest relationships.

In this chapter we consider the work of Bruce Perry (2009), who developed a neurosequential model of therapeutics based on the hierarchy of brain structure and function, and Jaak Panksepp's (2011) concept of a nested brain and mind hierarchy that explains how core emotions impact our cognitive processing. These perspectives underscore the reasons why early social experiences matter because they directly develop structures and functions (primary processes) that shape advanced development (secondary and tertiary processes). This is true not only because early social experiences provide the foundation, but because dynamically they also continue to exert influence through their interwoven nature.

In his seminal work on the relational brain, Daniel Siegel (1999, 2012) also talked about the hierarchical nature of the brain identifying what he terms *vertical integration*—a process that gathers information from the brain stem and limbic region into integration with the prefrontal cortex. Vertical integration leads to personal well-being and cooperative relationships, and it is one of the nine pathways of neural integration Siegel proposes, and so we discuss it in the next chapter within the overall context of integration.

Beginning with Perry and Panksepp, let's look more closely at these concepts to find out what is making it so difficult for Bobby to behave and to see what role play might have in changing his behavior.

Perry's Neurosequential Model

Bruce Perry's (1997; Perry & Szalavitz, 2006) main concern is demonstrating that early development matters greatly, and that the caretaking relationships of infancy and childhood determine, to a large extent, the core neurobiological organization of each individual. He uses a trapezoid shape (Figure 3.1) to designate four levels of the brain showing how it is organized from the brain stem, the sim-

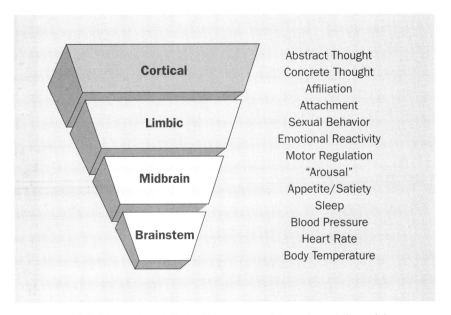

FIGURE 3.1. Hierarchy of Brain Structure and Function. Adapted from Perry (1997, 2009; Perry & Szalavitz, 2006). Copyright © Dec 25, 2007 Bruce Perry. Reprinted by permission of Basic Books, a member of the Perseus Book Group.

plest structure having the fewest cells, to the frontal cortex, the most complex with the most cells and the most synapses. On the right side of the figure is a list of the various corresponding functions of the brain, starting at the bottom with the simplest and most reflexive, the regulation of body temperature, to the most complex, abstract thought. The organization of each of these areas occurs during various stages of development (or in the process of making changes in the mature brain) in direct response to life experiences. Perry (1997) notes: "The more a certain neural system is activated, the more it will 'build in' this neural state—creating an internal representation of the experience corresponding to this neural activation. This use-dependent capacity to make internal representations of the external or internal world is the basis for learning and memory" (p. 128). He is writing about not only cognitive learning, but how we also encode and remember emotional and behavioral patterns. In fact, in the first 2 years of life, this emotionally and relationally based memory is the dominant form of learning.

Perry also says that the development of the brain is sequential, one layer building upon the other, thus the idea of a *neurosequential* model. He further introduces the idea that the capacity of a mature adult to regulate frustrations, impulsivity, aggression, and violent behavior depends on the full and sequential development of each layer in the brain. Perry emphasizes repeatedly that due to the neuroplasticity of the brain (the ability of the brain to reorganize itself by forming new neural connections throughout life), adults can alter their brain function throughout the lifespan. However, during infancy and childhood, experiences literally create the organizing framework of the brain.

We can begin to see that Bobby's impulsivity and aggression are deeply rooted in the way his brain organized itself in direct response to his early experiences of abandonment because of his mother's overwhelmed and unpredictable state. If we are born into a family of well-integrated adults, as infants we can "borrow" the helpful functions of our parents' prefrontal cortices to gradually co-create the neural structures that support empathy and the ability to make choices about our behaviors. This circuitry is quite complex. It draws together many different circuits and also potentially slows down the process sufficiently for us to make a choice other than the one dictated by fear. However, without these initial relational experiences, we don't develop these integrated pathways. When stress occurs, we are instantly catapulted to the core fight–flight nuclei in the brain stem for a very rapid response that precludes the time it takes to choose a different course.

This is Bobby's dilemma. However, he is not without hope. Neuroplasticity means that it is never too late to cultivate the regulatory circuitry within relationship, and attuned play activities do just that: They contribute crucially important experiences that stimulate and shape the development of these deep structures in the brain. We can gain a clear sense of this process as we integrate Perry's idea of hierarchy with Panksepp's notion that the seven core motivational systems, one of them being PLAY, are nested within all the layers of the brain.

Panksepp's Nested Brain Hierachy

Like Perry, Jaak Panksepp (Panksepp, 2011; Panksepp & Biven, 2012) believes that in order for higher mind and brain functions to operate effectively, they have to be fully integrated with the lower subcortical functions. He uses the concept of a nested hierarchy that is similar to Perry's neurosequential model. He developed the terminology of *MindBrain* and *BrainMind* (his caps) to emphasize how difficult it is to separate mind and body. Panksepp and Biven (2012) state:

> In the past, when an apparently healthy patient appeared emotionally agitated and complained of physical symptoms, doctors tended to believe that the symptoms were psychosomatic, "all in the mind," and therefore not physical or "real." This is no longer an accepted view of psychosomatic illness. As soon as we recognize that affects emerge from emotional systems that are fueled by brain chemicals that can also exert an eventual effect on the functioning of the brain and the body, then the division between emotional and physical disorders narrows to the point of extinction. Although it may appear that the mind and the brain are different entities, the mind being incorporeal, and the brain being physical, they are really one and the same thing. The MindBrain (or BrainMind) is a unified entity lacking any boundary with the body—it is integral to the physical system as a whole. (p. xiii)

Panksepp uses the term *MindBrain* when he is referring to top-down processing (the influence of the later developing structures on the earlier) and the term *BrainMind* for bottom-up processing (the influence of the earlier developing on the later). Panksepp's picture is of a two-way or "circular" causality among the three levels of his nested hierarchical concept. Panksepp and Biven (2012) use a triangular shape (Figure 3.2) to help us envision the evolutionary layers of the emotional processing in the BrainMind and to offer a different way of thinking about the origins of affective experience in the brain.

At the bottom of the figure, we see the primary-process instinctual emotions that generate raw feelings. Mother Nature builds these into our brains as "tools for living" (Panksepp & Biven, 2012, p. xii), and we begin at the bottom (where the seven primary motivational systems lie that we first explored in Chapter 1) because, according to Panksepp and Biven, this is the foundation of our affective consciousness. As we can see, Panksepp (2011) lists 3 different kinds of

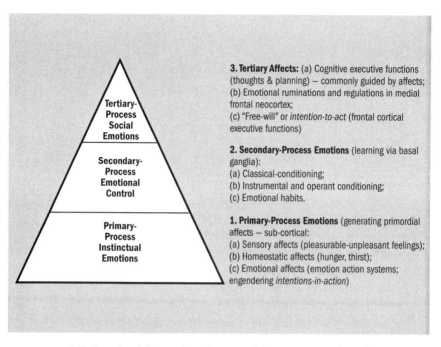

FIGURE 3.2. Levels of Control in Emotional Processing. Adapted from Panksepp (2011) and Panksepp and Biven (2012). "Figure 1.4," "Figure 1.6" from *The Archaeology of Mind: Neuroevolutionary Origins of Human Emotions* by Jaak Panksepp and Lucy Biven. Copyright © 2012 by Jaak Panksepp and Lucy Biven. Used by permission of W. W. Norton & Company, Inc.

primordial affects (sensory, homeostatic, and emotional affects). In the context of play therapy, we are particularly interested in the third type, also called "emotion action systems" because we can observe and work with these systems when they come online. Here we focus on several of these systems, but especially the PLAY action system. Ogden, Minton, and Pain (2006) draw from Panksepp's research to talk about the intertwining, yet separate nature of these action systems. For example, SEEKING (which they refer to as the "exploration action system" (pp. 114–115) often activates at the same time the PLAY system does, but they also acknowledge that these are separate action systems based on Panksepp's research providing evidence for neural circuitry that is unique for each action system as we discussed in Chapter 1.

Panksepp says that these primordial affects (motivational systems) engender "intentions-in-action" at the primary process level in contrast to the "intention-to-act" that occurs as *free will* at the tertiary level where frontal cortical executive functions are involved. What does this mean? Ogden, Minton and Pain (2006) give us a good description of how the *intentions-in-action*, or what they call "play signals" (p. 172), of the PLAY action system become visible to the therapist. They also suggest ways to engage this *play action system*, especially when working with trauma victims where this system is often initially disengaged because of lack of safety. They note,

> Play is often accompanied by specific 'play signals'—nonverbal gestures and postures such as increased eye contact, facial expression, spontaneous physical proximity, and enhanced social engagement (Beckoff & Byers, 1998). It is usually indicated by smiles, giggles, laughter, and other expressions of pleasure, fun, and social connectedness (Panksepp, 1998). Associated with comfort in one's sense of self, autonomy, and well-being, play arises spontaneously, and . . . is inhibited immediately by the threat of danger and fear. Therefore, the emergence of the play system indicates a relative absence of fear and defensive subsystems.
>
> The practice of psychotherapy must bring clients 'from a state of not being able to play into a state of being able to play' (Winnicott, 2005, p. 50). However, therapists may feel that they must stay focused exclusively on resolving the symptoms and difficulties that clients bring. Thus they may fail to recognize the health and vitality that can surface in moments of playfulness, humor, buoyancy, and resilience to otherwise distressing material, fostering a sense of overall well-being, if only for a moment. (pp. 172–173)

From this clinical description of how therapists might begin to engage with the PLAY action system (*intentions-in-action*, as Panksepp also describes it), we see why Panksepp has for a long time insisted on the importance of recognizing, from a scientific evidence base, that primary affects emerge from the bottom up, and not from the top down as so many other scientists have proposed. If we work only from the top down (where we often become overly focused on cognitive processes), we may miss the *play signals* that arise from the

bottom up in the form of spontaneous nonverbal gestures and p(
tures that reveal the intention to engage socially through play
(*intentions-in-action*).

The secondary-process emotions are pictured in the middle of
Figure 3.2 where learning and memory mechanisms include the
structures that mediate (1) classical conditioning, (2) instrumental
and operant conditioning, and (3) behavioral and emotional habits.
Here Panksepp and Biven (2012) give us another way to think about
classical learning theories. They believe that when we consider emotional learning, we need to "remember that emotional feelings are
integrally anchored to the emotional action systems of the brain" (p.
209). For example, they say that the experience of "FEAR itself" (p.
209)—an unconditioned response—greatly affects how conditioned
fears are learned in classical learning experiments in the first place,
and this fact is often overlooked. From Panksepp's and Biven's
(2012) perspective "the unconditioned emotional responses to environmental events are felt as 'rewards' and 'punishments' within the
brain" (p. 210). They provide a good example of this kind of learning
that is particularly relevant for our discussion.

> The PLAY system allows children to learn about the social rules
> of conduct—for example, when to cooperate and when to
> compete, and at times to retreat in good-humored ways and let
> someone else win. When animals engage in rough-and-tumble
> play and one animal wins more than 70% of the time, the los-
> ing animal no longer enjoys the game and may drop out of
> such interactions entirely. So when children play, they learn
> valuable social skills, such as the necessity of reciprocity and
> giving way on occasion. Children will learn these skills be-
> cause, if they do not, their playmates may begin to reject them.
> (p. xix)

In this example, the primary urge to PLAY is an emotional arousal
that is a reward when the child reciprocates, uses good humor, and
gives way to others, and it is punishment (if removed by the withdrawal of play by another child) when the child is too dominant,
competitive, or lacking in good humor. Children learn to approach
the behaviors that allow them to continue playing, and they avoid
the behaviors that cause their playmates to withdraw. For purposes
of illustration this example is no doubt oversimplified because surely

SEEKING and PANIC/GRIEF are also interwoven when children have bouts of play.

Tertiary affects at the top of the diagram include the wide range of cognitions and thoughts that allow us to reflect and to be aware of what we have learned from our emotional experiences (including our PLAY experiences). The tertiary social emotions include (1) executive cognitive functions (thoughts and planning that are often guided by affects), (2) emotional ruminations and regulations, and (3) our "free-will" or intention-to-act (Panksepp, 2011). At this level we are capable of developing and using the massive processing capacities of our cerebral cortices allowing us to make conscious decisions from our *free wills* to control our primary process emotions. For example, we may choose to delay responding to our PLAY urges (or some more complicated and intertwining version of that and other primary systems) because we have chosen (through cognitive executive functions) to act on some other competing need, e.g., to go to work because we need to earn money.

In contrast to cognitive scientists who continue to support the famous James–Lange theory that emotions are created when the neocortex reads them (*read-out theory*), Panksepp provides evidence from animal laboratory studies that "affective consciousness" is gen- erated in subcortical levels of the brain, as we see in Figure 3.2. The read-out theory of emotions implies that affective consciousness cannot come from the deep layers of the brain because these sub- strates are noncognitive. Panksepp suggests, however, that equating consciousness with cognition is simply not correct. Instead, he says that primary emotional systems (including PLAY) are nonlinguistic energetic forms of consciousness, what he terms *affective conscious- ness*. He points out that these primal feelings are built into our brains because they are so useful to us in dealing with the immediacy of what is happening in our environments. Panksepp and Biven (2012) summarize their position: "To the best of our knowledge, the basic biological values of all mammalian brains were built upon the same basic plan, laid out in consciousness-creating affective circuits that are concentrated in subcortical regions, far below the neocortical 'thinking' cap that is so highly developed in humans" (p. 1).

Panksepp (2011) points out that if we were to accept the James– Lange theory of emotions, we might then get the false impression that PLAY (one of the seven emotional systems) emerges from the neocortex. Panksepp (1998) dramatically demonstrated in his animal laboratory that this is just not the case. He asked research assistants to compare the behaviors of a normal group of playing rats with a group of playing rats whose cerebral cortices had been surgically removed (i.e., "decorticated"). The research assistants always mistook the invigorated and boisterous play of the rats without cerebral cortices to be normal while judging the subdued behaviors of the rats with intact normal brains to be less healthy (p. 308).

Panksepp and Biven (2012) provide further evidence of the subcortical origins of affective experience with human examples. Anencephalic babies (i.e., babies born without cerebral hemispheres), although remaining intellectually undeveloped, can grow up to be affectively vibrant children if they are raised in nurturing and socially engaging environments. They also point out that aphasic stroke victims (usually with left neocortical damage) maintain their affective capacity, indicating that affective consciousness is independent of language (p. 14).

From this evidence we can see that the cortex is simply not necessary for PLAY, even though it is often instrumental in developing sophisticated forms of play due to its large memory and processing capacities that allow us to hold and manipulate a wide range of play ideas and behaviors. One only has to think of the sophisticated game of chess to know that the processing power of the cortex is essential to some forms of play. The varied forms of play that we humans have invented, however, are not the same as the primary motivation to PLAY.

THE CORTEX AS THE PLAYGROUND OF THE MIND

This tension between cognitive scientists and affective neuroscientists reminds me of the struggles that Margaret Lowenfeld (originator of sand tray therapy) encountered with the conventional wisdom of her time that babies could not think because they did not have language (Lowenfeld, 1979/1993). She insisted that they could think, explaining that they just did not have words for reporting their nonverbal thought processes. We now know from research that babies *do* think, and perhaps this idea of "nonverbal thinking" that is so core to sand tray therapy is similar to this concept of "nonlinguistic affective consciousness" that Panksepp is suggesting.

Panksepp (1998) elaborates on the interwoven nature of the levels of emotional processing in the brain. He explains that even though decortication of rat brains does not eliminate PLAY motivation, play does seem to have powerful effects on the cortex. He explains: "One of the adaptive functions of juvenile play may involve programming various cortical functions. In a sense, the cortex may be the playground of the mind, and PLAY circuits may be a major coordinator of activities on that field of play" (p. 291). Using Panksepp's metaphor, we can see this playground of the cortex and the core programming of the PLAY system in Figure 3.2 in the brain's processing of emotions and affects.

We are taking the time to consider this hierarchy of emotional processing levels because it gives us a developmental perspective on why the social circuits of PLAY, CARE, and PANIC/GRIEF/Separation Distress are so critical early in life. During infancy and toddlerhood the primary-process instinctual emotions are very prominent. Infants have almost no control over their secondary or tertiary emotional processes, and relationships with others (and the brain processes they "lend") are necessary for them to learn how to use and regulate their primary emotions. As we mature into adulthood, the triangle is reversed, and we rely on higher mental processes (tertiary processes) to regulate our primary and secondary processes. Panksepp and Biven (2012) position the two triangles side by side (Figure 3.3) to point out how prominent the primary-process instinctual emotions are in early development, and conversely, how salient the tertiary-process social emotions are in maturity.

Panksepp's levels of emotional processing also depend on the sequencing of subcortical to cortical development. If we were fortunate early in life to experience our primary-process instinctual emotions within relationships that were co-regulating, we learned to interweave our levels of emotional processing in flexible and constructive ways, and we learned how to manage our raw emotions in socially acceptable ways. If we were really fortunate, we learned to live joyous lives by knowing how and when to use playfulness even during our most serious and challenging moments. The Dalai Lama is a master at using his playful spirit to navigate difficult situations.

Early experiences are often less than ideal, however. If we were a

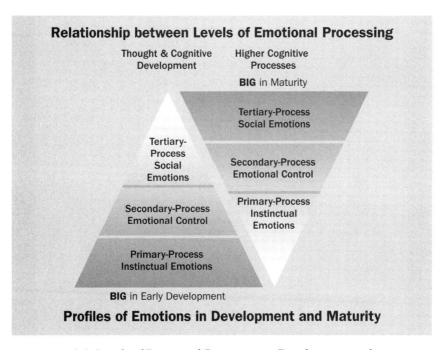

Relationship between Levels of Emotional Processing

Thought & Cognitive Development

Higher Cognitive Processes

BIG in Maturity

Tertiary-Process Social Emotions

Tertiary-Process Social Emotions

Secondary-Process Emotional Control

Primary-Process Instinctual Emotions

Secondary-Process Emotional Control

Primary-Process Instinctual Emotions

BIG in Early Development

Profiles of Emotions in Development and Maturity

FIGURE 3.3. Levels of Emotional Processing in Development and Maturity. Adapted from Panksepp and Biven (2012), p. 16. "Figure 1.4," "Figure 1.6" from *The Archaeology of Mind: Neuroevolutionary Origins of Human Emotions* by Jaak Panksepp and Lucy Biven. Copyright © 2012 by Jaak Panksepp and Lucy Biven. Used by permission of W. W. Norton & Company, Inc.

little less fortunate, or perhaps even unfortunate during our early years in learning how to interweave these levels of emotional processing, we can still change our mental systems and how we live, thanks to what we now know about the brain's lifelong neuroplasticity. We can always learn how to manage our emotional processing in ways that bring joy and satisfaction. Psychotherapy can be instrumental in helping patients engage their play action systems. Marks-Tarlow (2012) provides a beautiful description of how play cuts across all modalities, whether we are working with children or adults (in the playroom or not), to enhance the effectiveness of therapy. She notes:

> Whether or not we are conscious of using it, because play is a major source for implicit learning within the social domain, I

propose it as a nonspecific factor to therapeutic effectiveness that cross-cuts all modalities. Further, I suggest that play bears an important relationship to creativity, especially as it exists *in the intersubjective space between the therapist and patient.*

Sometimes clinicians sense the instinct to play coming to the fore, as when we consciously search for new possibilities with a lighthearted spirit or when we coconstruct safe experiments with patients to try at home or in the room. But more often play emerges implicitly, that is automatically, in bottom-up fashion, as a primary tool of clinical intuition. (p. 89)

Ogden et al. (2006) also talks about the importance of engaging the play action system as we help patients to expand their windows of tolerance. In my experience, this happens quite naturally in the playroom with children, and if we stay alert to the possibilities for playful moments with our adult patients, we can often help them to develop new neural pathways between the subcortical urges to play and the playground of the mind where we can use play to navigate the complexities of mature social relationships.

Although Panksepp and Perry both portray hierarchical levels in the brain, it is important to recognize that the layers do not correspond to each other in the two models. Perry is discussing primarily the *structural anatomy* and functions of the brain as it develops, whereas Panksepp is concerned with the *affective functioning* of the mind and how the three levels are related to each other. Both are saying that the levels are hierarchical *and* that the levels are integral to one another. Another way of saying this is that the top layers are not more or less important than the bottom layers, and in fact, the top layers cannot develop well without the adequate development of the other layers. Furthermore, there is a continuous influence of bottom-up processing throughout the lifespan, as well as the potential for a top-down capacity for regulation and self-control, when we receive the necessary relational support early in life or repair later in life.

Panksepp (2011) illustrates this concept as a *nested* BrainMind hierarchy in Figure 3.4. It is clear from the arrows in the diagram that the influences of the levels of relationship within the nested hierarchy are two-way, both bottom-up and top-down processing. Panksepp refers to this as "circular" causation. He explains:

In order for higher MindBrain functions to mature and function (via bottom-up control), they have to be integrated with the lower BrainMind functions, with primary-processes being depicted as squares (red), secondary-process learning as circles (green), and tertiary processes, by rectangles (blue). Panksepp uses color coding to convey the manner in which nested hierarchies integrate lower brain functions into higher brain functions to eventually exert top-down regulatory control.[1] (p. 6)

Returning to our example of Bobby, we can use Panksepp's triangle (Figure 3.2) and his nested hierarchy (Figure 3.4) to see how the raw emotions (SEEKING, RAGE, FEAR, CARE, PANIC/GRIEF, and PLAY[2]) of Bobby's early development reside (are nested) within his cortical processing. His capacity to regulate his behavior is influenced by what the primary processes bring to the neocortex, and we can see just how vulnerable he is to behaving inappropriately. Because his early care was inconsistent, sometimes abusive, and

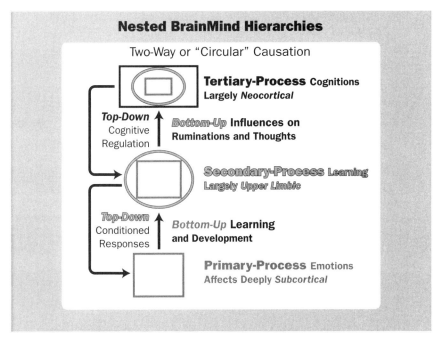

FIGURE 3.4. Panksepp's Nested BrainMind Hierarchy. Reprinted with permission from Panksepp (2011).

often lacking relational attunement, his many unresolved and unregulated emotional feelings are an integral part of his cortical processing (primary-process emotions nested in the top layer). Bobby was not able to develop and learn a consistent strategy (secondary processes) for handling his social–emotional relationships. His behavioral decisions (tertiary processes) fall apart so easily in response to so many little triggers.

One of the ways the cortex is influenced by early subcortical development is that with many repetitions of experience, we develop what are called *cortical invariant representations* that further cement in our subcortical, affective learnings (Hawkins & Blakeslee, 2004). In Bobby's case, these invariant representations might include that he is a bad boy or that he can't control himself. These representations now form a big circle with the concomitant subcortical upset, leading to more of the same kind of behavior. With insufficient linkages between the subcortical and cortical circuitry because of his early relationships, there is little chance that his own brain processes can allow him to intervene to make a change, particularly when he has both an implicitly and cortically stacked deck. In relationship with Dr. Matthews, this new circuitry can be supported in its development.

In the next chapter we're going to turn our attention to two frameworks that can help us better sense the possible outcomes of the structure and function co-created by mother and child early in life: complexity theory and the pathways of neural integration. Our story of Bobby continues as we look at these brain processes.

CHAPTER NOTES

1. Panksepp's nested hierarchy figure is available in color in his PLoS One (2011) online article.

2. We did not include LUST here because the activation of this system generally comes into play in adolescence.

Chapter 4

COMPLEXITY AND NEURAL INTEGRATION ON THE ROAD TO MENTAL HEALTH

Daniel Siegel (2012) offers some indicators of the brain's unfolding healing process that can help us track the emergence of mental health in the playroom. Our brains are always seeking greater integration and coherence as part of their inherent developmental process. In play, we can experience and observe an initially chaotic or rigid system move toward coherence when obstacles are removed naturally through being given space for expression within the relationship. As neural integration emerges, we can further refine our "seeing" by becoming aware of the nine domains that Siegel identifies, giving us a way to track a young child's developmental unfolding as we did with Bobby in the last chapter. *Complexity theory* and *pathways of integration* can serve as guiding frameworks from which we can derive principles for how we can best use our presence and how we may understand and support what this child is doing in our playrooms.

COMPLEXITY THEORY AT WORK IN A COMPLICATED LIFE

A "complicated life" describes Bobby's situation well even though he is only 9 years old. He is a delightful child who can, in a flash, become aggressive and behave impulsively. This struggle with regulation actually indicates that his brain development was impeded on its journey toward complexity by the hindrances created in his tumultuous early relational life. Complex systems such as the brain are self-organizing, which means they have a built-in tendency to move toward coherence through a process in which differentiated circuits are drawn into connection with one another, leading to a more integrated and better functioning system. In the brain this growth toward complexity takes us in the direction of greater well-being and warm relationships (Siegel, 1999, 2012). However, when early relationships (often), stressors in the environment (unsafe neighborhood, natural disaster—sometimes), or genetic mishaps (rarely) throw up roadblocks, that natural movement toward integration is hindered in some areas, and our capacity for empathic relationships, regulation, and choosing our behavior is compromised a little or a lot.

Complexity theory is worth our attention because it provides useful ways for us to sense where we and our clients are along the continuum toward coherence. Daniel Siegel (1999, 2007, 2012; Siegel & Bryson, 2011) offers a picture of a "river of coherence" flowing down the middle, with rigidity on one bank and chaos on the other. Early chaotic lives have a tendency to leave our brains unintegrated in ways that render us easily vulnerable to stress. When our environment pushes on this inner structure, we are most apt to react with a big release of energy without a coherent pattern—as happens often for Bobby. The neural circuitry between the subcortical and cortical areas is not linked in a way that helps him calm down or even seek the help of others. Chaos overflows with spontaneity to the detriment of stability.

Another child, raised in an emotionally arid but intellectually solid household, often will shift into more cerebral, left-hemisphere functioning to stay connected to his or her parents. The result is often a powerful sense that rules matter, accompanied by firm standards of right–wrong, and a tendency for figuring out who's to blame. Emotional connection is replaced by a valuing of competence and strict behavioral standards, a pretty hollow bargain. At the neurobiological level, there is a profound disconnection between the two hemispheres. In terms of the river, rigidity sacrifices flexibility and spontaneity for stability.

One way to track movement toward integration is to see in ou selves and our young ones a gradual shift from chaos toward regula tion or from rigidity toward more flexibility in behavior and warmer relatedness. We are then moving toward the middle of the river where there's just enough stability to create a sense of safety and abundant room for creative spontaneity without falling into chaos. How this coherence looks for each individual is unique, but the feeling of this movement is unmistakable. One hallmark is a greater playfulness as the sense of safety through connection gains strength. On this foundation, let's spend a little time looking at the specifics of complexity theory.

Principle 1: Brains–Minds Are Self-Organizing, from Levels of Simplicity to Complexity

The first principle of complexity theory says that there is a genetically driven natural push throughout our lives to move from simplicity toward complexity. Siegel (2012) cites an example of a child developing increasingly sophisticated abilities such as reaching, crawling, and then walking. These patterns of increasing complexity emerge naturally in children as a result of their interactions with the environment. This push toward complexity is so natural that we often take it for granted unless, of course, there is some hindrance or barrier inhibiting this flow. For the most part, there is no way to stop this flow of emerging patterns of increasing complexity. It begins at conception and stays with us as backdrop throughout our entire lives over a number of different contexts, including play.

Some of the development of babies is largely genetically driven and truly self-organizing, such as the developmental steps involved in the journey from crawling to running and jumping, cited above. However, many abilities are more "co-organizing" (or we could say that the mother–child system is self-organizing) at the beginning, as it takes mother and child to create the relational dance for the emergence of neural integration. Using a simple game that mothering people[1] play with their babies, we can see this co-organizing principle at work. "I'm gonna getcha" is a good example of how mothering people naturally support and encourage this tendency to move toward ever-increasing complexity. The mother uses a simple finger-march up the baby's belly to get the baby's attention, and if the baby responds positively, the game is repeated over and over with lots of laughter and mutual delight.

You might wonder how this repetition could create so much delight. If you watch carefully, however, you will notice that each repetition has a slight variation (since babies habituate quickly), and soon there is a complex set of variations in how mother and baby respond to each other. The second finger-march might be a little slower with the mother's voice a little softer. Then you might see a quickening of the gonna-getcha-march with the mother's eyes opening wider, her lips parting slightly, and her voice a little more excited. The baby responds with a look of anticipation and then a squeal of delight when her mother's fingers reach her neck for a gentle tickle. You might see both the mother's and the baby's heads turning this way or that signaling more or less play. The endless variations on this type of play create an increasingly complex set of interactions between mother and baby as they develop their social–emotional relationship. On the surface, it looks quite natural and simplistic, but when studied in frame-by-frame detail, as Stern (1977/2002) and others have done, we can see a very complex set of relational signals developing between the mothering person and the child.

Unfortunately for Bobby, there were few opportunities for this kind of co-organization to take place in a positive manner through playful interactions. The brain's natural drive toward some kind of organization is still present, however, so instead of a highly complex and stable system of secure attachment between mother and baby, we find a child who is frequently thwarted when his SEEKING system caused him to reach out or call out to his mother for nurturing and playful interactions. Since Bobby's attempts to connect were frequently thwarted, pain and fear arose in him initially and became shame by his second year. His natural drive to reach out is now linked to rejection and feelings of wrongness. Sometimes his mother did play with him, even if she did not always attune well, and so the further element of unpredictability is added to his organization of what it means to be in a human relationship. As we will see, children like Bobby can benefit when these kinds of hindrances to their innate tendency to move toward healing, wholeness, and collaborative relationships are removed, a process that unfolds in a relationally rich environment.

Principle 2: Complex Systems Are Nonlinear: Small Changes, Large Effects

This principle means that small changes in one part of the system can create large changes in the entire system. Our brains encode our experiences in neural nets that literally gather up all aspects into one firing pattern (Hebb, 1949). When current-day experience tugs on one thread of any experience, there is some probability that the entire experience will be activated, with the sense of a much larger response than the original stimulus seems to warrant. Bobby might hear a tone of voice that is familiar, and in that tug on one strand of an old memory, the entire neural net of rage might fly open. To others, his reaction appears to be much larger than expected. On the other hand, sometimes the smallest gesture of kindness can have a much larger than expected influence as well.

One such response happened to Bobby in the course of his treatment. Bobby's father had asked Dr. Matthews to speak to the school principal with whom Bobby was frequently in trouble. Weeks later, at the beginning of his play therapy session, Bobby's father reported that he was not getting in trouble as much at school. Dr. Matthews asked Bobby what was making it better at school. He replied, "Mr. Johnson [school principal] was nice to me. He asked me how I was doing." Although this single incident probably did not account for all of what was helping Bobby's behavior improve at school, it was the moment that stood out in his mind. We can imagine that perhaps it may have been the small shift of attention from the principal after his father and Dr. Matthews talked that created this greater than expected impact. When we are expecting one response (usually negative) and instead receive a different, whole-hearted interaction, large changes in our relational expectations and behavior can occur (Ecker, Ticic, Hulley, & Niemeyer, 2012).

Principle 3: Complex Systems Are Both Emergent and Recursive

This principle means that we are constantly experiencing states we've never felt before, and that these states are also influenced both by what we have already experienced and the environment around us. Siegel (2012) explains:

We are always in the natural state of being created and creating ourselves. We will never be the same, and we have never
been quite the way we are right at this moment. This emergence of being as we flow from state to state is characterized
by an underlying sense that there is an incredible amount of
both freedom and cohesion within the system in a given moment. As a person's states of mind emerge in ways determined
by the system's own internal constraints and by the external
constraints of interpersonal connections with others, the self is
perpetually being created. (p. 201)

Siegel also says that one of the ways that we as individuals or
within relationships experience emergence is when we enter a
bottom-up experience of attending to what is unfolding in this
moment. Likewise, recursive or repeating patterns of our emerging
states can bring us a sense of familiarity or predictability through
top-down experiences. In essence, the behavioral output (or flow) of
the system tends to feed back on itself to reinforce its direction even
while new information is beginning to shift the river to some degree.
The possibility for the emergence of coherence, chaos, and rigidity
resides here, as too much newness without the stability of the familiar can create chaos, whereas too much top-down familiarity without an influx of the new can lead to a deadening rigidity. In the
interplay of the two lies the stream of coherence.

Again, we can imagine some of Bobby's early experiences as an
infant to explore how these emergent and recursive features look in
a specific person. As Bobby's brain developed in relationship with his
mother's brain, he most likely behaved frequently in ways that were
quite disorganized due to the immaturity of his baby brain's circuitry
(emergent in the moment experience), and later due to his fragmented set of unpredictable experiences with his mother (both
emergent and recursive). His behavioral output would then elicit
further disorganized behavior (recursive) from his fragmented
mother, reinforcing this increasingly chaotic relationship. On the
other hand, when we imagine our "gonna-getcha" baby girl and her
highly attuned mother playing together, we can see that the baby
girl's delighted responses would elicit more play from her mother,
reinforcing the development of their ever-increasing set of subtle
signs and behaviors that help them create their relationship. New

movements in this co-organizing dance continue to emerge and feed into this delightfully co-reinforcing spiral of delight. This little girl learns over time what it means to be in a joyful, secure, and emotionally satisfying relationship.

A COMPLICATED LIFE AT PLAY

In the context of play, how would complexity theory be useful? The underlying theme in this theory, as well as what we have explored in the hierarchical ideas of Perry and Panksepp, is the concept of integration. How do we encourage all the parts to function together so that we can thrive? How does play help us thrive?

Let's return to Bobby. He loves his play therapy sessions with Dr. Matthews. He is especially attracted to the sand tray, and he uses it almost exclusively. In his beginning sessions, he builds a number of train wrecks in the sand. At first, it looks like he is stuck in repetitive play, but careful observation reveals a number of rich variations on his train-wreck theme. The scenes are always carefully constructed, week after week, each with a touch of artistry that makes them quite appealing. Then week after week, just as everything is perfectly set up, there is a sudden and terrible train wreck. A tornado comes, or the signal lights get mixed up, or the engineer is careless. An angry monster digs up the tracks just as the train approaches.

From complexity theory and the core idea of integration, Dr. Matthews could see that Bobby was using scenes in the sand to explore the many variations of his dysregulating life experiences. In the sudden wrecks, she could see the onset of chaos and the out-of-proportion response to a sometimes small input. She did not see him as "stuck in his play" because she could see his natural push toward self-organization revealing itself in the differences that emerged, as though Bobby were showing Dr. Matthews different perspectives on this underlying theme of wreckage. Dr. Matthews allowed him to lead with his play as she reflected in attuned ways, always mindful of her own regulation. If she felt small ripples of anxiety arising in her, she took a few deep breaths to return her own system to calmness. She carefully tracked his feelings, and she could see shifts in his behaviors. The similar-themed play within the relationship was gradually increasing his capacity for warm connection as well as his tolerance for frustration. Bobby could feel her CARE as she witnessed and held his PLAY.

Remembering that differentiation often precedes integration, Dr. Matthews took careful note of Bobby's play one day when he set up a switch on the tracks where the engineer could make a decision to go left or right. He made a sign for the left-bearing track that said "Bad Way" and another sign for the right one, "Good Way." Along the tracks of the "Bad Way" he placed scary things—monsters, spooky trees, and skeletons. For the "Good Way" he chose a rainbow, several smiley faces, some beautiful trees, and a pleasant house. Then he drove the train repeatedly over the tracks approaching the switch numerous times, sometimes choosing the "Bad Way" and sometimes choosing the "Good Way."

From this play, Dr. Matthews predicted (to herself), that Bobby's behavior would soon improve based on her awareness that this change in play likely represented a new linkage of parts that were allowing him to imagine that there might be a different way to approach his world than the one that had been guiding his behavior for so long. She was not disappointed. Several weeks later, Bobby's father reported how much easier the morning and bedtime routines had become. He also said Bobby had developed some friendships at school, and he seemed to be a lot more cooperative overall.

With complexity theory and the core idea of integration giving her wise eyes with which to view Bobby's play, Dr. Matthews could facilitate the unfolding process by reflecting and offering a gentle nudge here or there without becoming overly directive. Although parents and clinicians sometimes need to be directive in the context of play, with Bobby it was not necessary and probably would have impeded his progress since he had so often been forced out of his developmental pathway by his parents' difficulties. In honoring the innate wisdom of his own path, Dr. Matthews was also helping Bobby learn to trust himself.

THE PATHWAYS OF INTEGRATION

Using Siegel's (2012) idea of integration as a marker of healthy mental functioning, we can use play as a means to *recognize, rely on,* and *reinforce* the tendency of the brain's push toward wholeness. I call these the three R's of integrating play. Our own awareness of how brains integrate and minds become coherent helps us gain a felt sense for when something playful or some play activity is pushing toward integration.

To illustrate the three R's, let's talk about Elsie, a young adolescent girl who is playing with clay. She becomes increasingly animated as she smashes her fist into it, then picks it up and slaps it down hard on the table. With a kitchen knife she slashes it this way and that, then squishes the segments back together. Knowing that her mother has been very ill and unavailable due to her fight with cancer, and knowing that she can't talk about it, I *recognize* that her vigorous play gives her an appropriate container for her FEAR, RAGE, and the GRIEF/PANIC/Separation Distress of losing the experience of her healthy, available mother. Because I am aware of her brain's push toward wholeness, I can *rely on* this girl's growing edge to do what is best and most efficient for her to heal. We all have a growing edge regardless of whether or not our life situations are going well. The growing edge is that dynamic part of us that is always meeting up with new things, new feelings, new situations, and figuring out what to do with the new. Providing a free and protected space for Elsie, I can confidently *rely on* her natural capacity to engage in just the right thing.

I *reinforce* her play by staying present with her, making conscious decisions to attune to her, and trusting that these interpersonal offerings will be received by her because I know that we are constantly rewiring one another's brains. I am practicing mindfulness as well as drawing on my knowledge of complexity theory to collaborate with the way her mind (as a human system) is developing.

I am also quietly tracking my felt sense (right hemisphere) and conscious awareness (left hemisphere) of how the specific domains of integration are unfolding. Drawing together many strands of research, Daniel Siegel (2006, 2010, 2012) offers us a picture of our brain's nine main pathways of integration (Figure 4.1). We are going to use these pathways to see how they emerge in the course of a young adolescent girl involved in play therapy.

We are going to explore how we can recognize opportunities to support and nudge integration during the flow of the play therapy relationship by using these pathways. At times, the pathways of integration are overlapping and not always easy to identify as iso-

Daniel Siegel's Nine Pathways of Integration

Integration of Consciousness: Using awareness to create change and choice.

Interpersonal Integration: Connecting intimately in relationship while retaining our own sense of identity and freedom.

Vertical Integration: Linking together information from the body proper, the subcortical circuits (brainstem and limbic areas), and the prefrontal circuits in the right hemisphere and the cognitive awareness of the left hemisphere.

Memory Integration: Bringing the free-floating puzzle pieces of the past (implicit memories) into explicit awareness.

State Integration: Embracing the diverse states of being that embody our fundamental drives and needs, such as closeness and solitude, autonomy and independence, caregiving and mastery, among others.

Horizontal Integration: Linking and balancing the right hemisphere (early developing, rich in the realm of imagery, holistic thinking, nonverbal language, autobiographical memory, and other processes) with the left hemisphere (later developing, responsible for logic, spoken and written language, linearity, lists, and literal thinking).

Narrative Integration: Weaving our left hemisphere's narrator function with the autobiographical memory storage of our right hemisphere. The "we" of well-being.

Temporal Integration: Finding comforting connections in the face of uncertainty, impermanence, and immortality.

Transpirational Integration: Breathing across; awareness of being part of a larger whole.

FIGURE 4.1. Siegel's Pathways of Integration. Adapted from Siegel (2010, 2012).

lated categories, but our effort here is to deepen our awareness of emerging integration so that we can collaborate with it as it unfolds naturally. In the following clinical story of Elsie, a 13-year-old, we are tracking the pathways of integration by identifying them in numerical order, as seen in Figure 4.1, and then illustrating and the specific pathways in the clinical story.

PLAY THERAPY WITH ELSIE, 13-YEAR-OLD GIRL
Supporting Therapeutic Moments
of Potential Integration

Elsie is in therapy due to anxiety caused by her mother's life-threatening brain cancer that necessitated a series of radiation treatments. Over the past 6 months, her mother has been unable to manage the household, and a part-time caretaker is helping with cleaning, some of the cooking, and child care for Elsie and her 7-year-old brother. Elsie was doing exceptionally well in school academically and socially until shortly after her mother became ill. Elsie has a difficult time talking about her mother's illness, and when the topic comes up in therapy, she says it is not really bothering her that much because she knows her mother has a good medical team. Her parents are concerned because her grades are suffering, and she seems to be withdrawing from her friends.

FOUNDATIONAL PILLARS OF CHANGE

1. *Integration of Consciousness*: Using awareness to create change and choice.
2. *Interpersonal Integration*: Connecting intimately in relationship while retaining our own sense of identity and freedom.

As we consider what is happening as Elsie plays with the sand tray and then clay, we will begin with the first pathways of integration: *integration of consciousness* and *interpersonal integration*. When the therapist is able to offer an open, nonjudgmental, mindful space in the playroom, that mindfulness is an expression of integrated consciousness. Because we are constantly influencing one another's neural firing patterns, when patients come into a mindful space, there is a felt sense of safety and their brains begin to rewire in patterns similar to the therapist's. In safety, play can reach into the patient's experiences of hurt or fear and bring these affective experiences into the relational space between therapist and patient. When both patient and therapist are holding these old pains and fears together, that is *interpersonal integration*. The relationship becomes the means of healing as he or she is seen, heard, understood, and comforted. In the process, the patient's own sense of self has space to emerge as well. We might consider these two forms of integration the foundational pillars of change.

When Elsie first came to therapy, she engaged intensely in making sand trays, and she spent a lot of time creating scenes of conflict (e.g., a school dance where friends got into a fight, and a scene with a fence dividing a group of peaceful animals in a meadow from a wild and threatening monster). I witnessed these conflicts in an interested but nonjudgmental way. Within this relational process, safety began to emerge and she was able to present her internal conflicts to me in metaphors, showing me what was so painful inside her without having to use words.

I reflected what little she told me about the scenes, and I refrained from asking her questions because I felt pretty sure that she did not yet feel safe in the verbal realm. Elsie seemed to understand that I would allow her to set the pace. She enjoyed coming to therapy, and she continued to show me how distressed she felt in the images of the sand tray. I could hold these painful images without asking her to do anything with them cognitively. I wanted to hold a space with her where she could process her emotions at primary and secondary levels. From awareness of Panksepp's nested hierarchy, I believed that taking the time for this subcortical processing would create the foundation for cognitive understanding to emerge later in therapy.

3. *Vertical Integration*: Linking together information from the body proper, the subcortical circuits (brainstem and limbic areas), and the prefrontal circuits in the right hemisphere and the cognitive awareness of the left hemisphere.
4. *Memory Integration*: Bringing the free-floating puzzle pieces of the past (implicit memories) into explicit awareness.
5. *State Integration*: Embracing the diverse states of being that embody our fundamental drives and needs, such as close-

ness and solitude, autonomy and dependence, caregiving and mastery, among others.

Safety in relationship opened the door to the next pathway—*vertical integration*—which means drawing information from the body, the subcortical circuits, and the prefrontal circuits in the right hemisphere into relationship and eventually into conscious awareness. Two additional kinds of integration—*memory and state*—are part of this process.

As Elsie felt increasingly safe, she was able to move from the sand tray into playing vigorously with clay. Her angry feelings and strong physical expression were part of her implicit (embodied) memory of what it was like for her mother to be so ill and unavailable to her. Prior to expression, these feelings were trapped in her body and subcortical circuitry, not connected to the resources of regulation and so easily triggered by any implication that she was not at her best.

At the beginning of one session, Elsie's mother asked to speak to me outside the door of the waiting room. Sensing how distraught she was, I agreed and then realized immediately that Elsie needed to be in on this conversation because the mother wanted to talk about her fears concerning Elsie's performance at school. I asked the mother to come inside into the private waiting area so that we could include Elsie in the discussion to see if I could help them resolve (or at least clarify) the mother's concerns. In retrospect, I recognized my therapeutic error in agreeing at first to speak to the mother without Elsie. But it was too late! During the rest of the session in the playroom, Elsie managed to get a lot of sand caught in her rolled-up sleeves, and numerous times she managed to shake the sand onto the floor from the sleeves of her shirt. This was unusual behavior for her, and I could see that she was angry. Toward the end of the session, I told her that it must have been very hard for her to learn that her mother and I had been talking about her outside the door of the waiting room when they first arrived. I said, "I didn't know that your mother wanted to talk with me about your grades. That is why I asked your mother to come inside so we could talk. I thought you should be in on that discussion."

I was trying to repair, to reestablish interpersonal integration, but I could see that it was difficult for her to accept. So I said, "It must have been really hard to talk about your grades when you are trying so hard to do your best. I can understand that you might be pretty angry with me." Although Elsie did not overtly confirm her feelings of anger toward me, it did seem to shift something in the therapy. It was in the following session that she elected to move from the sand tray to the clay area where she was able to physically express her anger through vigorous bodily movement in the safety of playing with clay. This physical expression allowed her to move toward *vertical integration* by bringing the feeling out of hiding into her body, emotions, and conscious awareness.

As she was able to access these memories (memories of anger that had been denied) in my presence, our joint attention allowed Elsie's prefrontal circuitry to make new connections with the subcortical circuits, leading to a gradual change in behavior (*memory integration*). Elsie found the clay comforting, and she chose to work with it over the following six sessions. At first she made grotesque objects—an overly large spider with beady eyes, a three-headed monster with vampire teeth, a wild and "evil" cat, a mask with hollow eyes, and finally a skeleton complete with casket.

Although Elsie played vigorously with the clay, she stayed organized in her use of the materials, and once she reached the depth of despair in the metaphor of the casket, she began to create objects with a very different feel. She announced this turn of events one day when she entered the playroom. Walking directly to the clay table, she said, "I'm not going to make any more death stuff." Although she did not verbally say as much, she was showing me that she was now able to access the denied memories and embrace her state of deep anger about her mother's illness—*memory integration* and *state integration*. Elsie proceeded to mold a little sports car that she painted red and then made a gas station (metaphorically providing energy for her vehicle, herself). Soon after, she created a vase with flowers followed by a plate of fruit.

Another way we store old painful feelings is through different states of mind. As she was smashing the clay, I could see how Elsie's felt sense of abandonment (one state of mind) had come into conflict with loving her mother (another state of mind), creating intolerable stress that was now being released through her strong bodily movements. These two states could begin to move toward resolution—*state integration*.

6. *Horizontal Integration*: Linking and balancing the right hemisphere (early developing, rich in the realm of imagery, holistic thinking, nonverbal language, autobiographical memory, and other processes) with the left hemisphere (later developing, responsible for logic, spoken and written language, linearity, lists, and literal thinking).

7. *Narrative Integration*: Weaving our left hemisphere's narrator function with the autobiographical memory storage of our right hemisphere.

After several rounds of smashing clay and other highly energized activities, Elsie began to be able to talk about how frightened she was at what was happening with her mother. She eventually was even able to speak about the sense of disloyalty and guilt she felt when she needed more of her mother's time and attention because she knew how sick she was. These are examples of *horizontal integration* (also called *bilateral integration)* and *narrative integration*. Often, after our young ones have done a powerful piece of work, the memories and states that are becoming integrated in the right hemisphere now begin to naturally move toward words in the left hemisphere. This movement across the hemispheres in either direction is bilateral integration, and the result is a new narrative that can be spoken for the first time.

In any healing process, we will cycle along these pathways again and again. At times, I could not hold such a mindful space—getting sick, tired, the normal inattentiveness of being human—and needed to repair with Elsie, reestablishing interpersonal integration. As we will see when we explore attachment in the next chapter, the hallmark of secure attachment is rupture and repair rather than a steady state of connection—something that can relieve our fears about not being a good-enough therapist when we falter. For her part, Elsie would rest a bit after doing a powerful piece of integration and expressing it in narrative, and then she would plunge into the next area in need of vertical integration, a new area of pain and fear, which she accomplished primarily through play held within our relationship. She would then work her way through her feelings until the new narrative attached to this part of her experience began to emerge.

8. *Temporal Integration*: Finding comforting connections in the face of uncertainty, impermanence, and immortality.

Over time, Elsie was able to talk more about her mother's illness, and though difficult, she was able to talk about the possibility that her mother might not recover. She continued to work with the clay and she also resumed building sand trays on occasion. Eventually her mother's treatment was successful, but because Elsie's developing brain was acquiring the prefrontal ability to sense the passing of time and the reality of death, she had a new awareness of mortality. She spoke with sadness about her new knowledge that she could lose a close family member, or that even she could get sick and die. But she also was able to say that she knew it was important to be grateful for all the fun times her family had when they did things together. Though young, she seemed willing to accept the comforts of being close with her family, indicating beginning steps toward *temporal integration*.

Transpirational integration often does not naturally emerge in the therapy process, but may appear as part of contemplative or mindfulness practice at some stage of our lives. However, being able to observe movement along the eight pathways of integration may give us a sense of where we are in the therapy process, steadying us, and that brings a sense of stability and calm into the room as part of the containing field for our young ones.

We will visit these pathways again in Parts II and III when we talk more about practical applications and treatment planning. As we will see, these pathways of integration are useful in a practical sense to guide decision-making as we attempt to collaborate with the way the brain–mind works (and plays) in therapy.

CHAPTER NOTE

1. I am borrowing Bonnie Badenoch's (2011) term *mothering people* with her permission because it includes both genders as well as aunts and uncles, and it seems softer and more personal than the term *caretaker*.

Chapter 5

BECOMING PART
OF OUR CHILDREN

There Was a Child Went Forth

His own parents,
He that had father'd him, and she that had conceiv'd
    him in her womb, and birth'd him,
They gave this child more of themselves than that;
They gave him afterward every day—they became part
    of him.

                —Walt Whitman, *Leaves of Grass*

We become part of our children, and they become part of us in a process we call *attachment*. How does it happen? And why does play matter as we form these early bonds with our children? The mental health field has been interested in attachment theory and research since John Bowlby (1969) first introduced the idea that children need more than good physical care to thrive, but there has been little discussion about what role play might have in nurturing and caring for the deep emotional needs that we each have at birth.

    Panksepp (2009) gives us a unique window into how PLAY and the other emotional systems present in us at birth (RAGE, FEAR, PANIC/GRIEF/Separation Distress, CARE, LUST, and SEEKING) serve as "ancestral tools for living" (p. 4). Although we have potential for developing these emotional systems in highly sophisticated ways through learning and cognitive processing, the actual circuits of these systems lie deep in the brain below the neocortex, and they do not need cognitive resources to become active. We have only to witness the rage of a hungry infant or to listen to her soft cooing as she gazes deeply into her mother's eyes to sense that this is so.

PLAY, as we have already discovered, begins very early, for some even before birth when their eager parents play with them rhythmically or vocally with gentle touch and song through the mother's abdomen. Others wait for the tongue-sticking-out play to which infants respond even on the first day of life. An infant's ability to imitate this tongue play (Dobbs, 2006) is due to the resonating properties of the brain and nervous system that lie at the heart of our capacity and our need for interpersonal integration. It is not just the infant's need for connection that motivates these playful interactions. Caregivers need these connections also as each of us remains an attachment-seeking being throughout our lifespan. Recently, a friend of mine spoke to me with eyes glistening about his grandson's response to the tongue play that he had initiated with him. He was deeply touched that his newborn grandson could already connect. He also said that the deep gazing from his grandson's eyes within hours of his birth was a soul-stirring experience.

Since Bowlby's time, a great deal of research has been done on attachment. From the work of Mary Ainsworth (Ainsworth, Blehar, Waters, & Wall, 1978), followed by Mary Main (1996, 2000) and others, we have methods for categorizing and assessing the different styles of attachment. In children, these styles fall into secure and three flavors of insecure (ambivalent, avoidant, or disorganized) patterns. The Adult Attachment Interview (AAI) assesses the adult's state of mind with regard to attachment, reflecting particular organizational patterns or engrained states of mind that began developing in the first year of life (Siegel, 2012). Although these research studies and assessment methods are important in our understanding of how human relationships develop, an in-depth review of this extraordinary body of research is beyond the scope of this book. Instead, we will touch lightly on the different styles of attachment in relation to the role of PLAY, as it is interwoven with the other primary emotional systems of CARE, SEEKING, and PANIC/GRIEF/

Separation Distress that promote attachment behaviors (or signal their absence) between infants and mothering people.

Panksepp (2009) gives us a unique way of understanding the attachment process by describing the emotional systems of CARE and PANIC/GRIEF/Separation Distress as the Janus-faced twins of deep social attachments (p. 14). He explains how their shared chemistries, especially the presence or absence of oxytocin and endogenous opioids, influence our relationships with others. He also says that PLAY has a remarkable effect on programming the cortex to become fully social. Let's review each of these systems, keeping in mind their dynamic interweaving as infants and mothering people develop their social attachments. We also include the SEEKING system because it serves as a generalized substrate for all the other emotional processes (see Figure 2.2).

"Nurturing Love" is the title Panksepp and Biven (2012) give to their chapter on the CARE system. They begin:

> Mammals would not exist on the face of the earth unless their brains and bodies were prepared to invest enormous time and energy in the care of their offspring, who simply could not survive without such devotion. The investment of maternal attention has not been left to chance: It is grounded in a solid set of instinctual brain urges to nurture newborn infants and to bond with them. (p. 283)

These maternal instincts become active prior to birth, in response to hormonal changes that involve increasing estrogen, prolactin, and oxytocin, while progesterone decreases. These hormonal changes have the potential to prepare the mother for the arrival of the infant, increasing her maternal devotion and sensitizing her brain to the pleasurable aspects of caring for a helpless infant. If the mother's internal world and the outer environment are favorable for mother and infant, they will form a secure bond. However, even with the presence of this inborn system and its powerful neurochemistry, some mothers do not experience this joyous expectancy. If there have been significant attachment losses or traumas, the mother's encoded experiences of pain and fear may override these systems, leaving her in a state of anxiety, depression, confusion, or even anger about the arrival of this little one, through no fault of her own.

However, her little one's instinctual nature is also prepared to reach toward Mother through his or her PANIC/GRIEF/Separation Distress system. "Born to Cry" is the chapter title Panksepp and Biven give to this emotional system, explaining that it is often the distress calls of the infant that bring the caring person to alleviate the panic and grief of being separated from sources of love and nurturance. Many parents speak about their unbidden movement toward their infant at the first sounds of distress as these two interlocking systems amplify one another. In the words of Panksepp and Biven (2012), this system is the "genesis of life-sustaining social bonds" (p. 311).

If CARE is not forthcoming in consistent and predictable ways in response to this distress, infants will form insecure bonds with their caregivers. For example, when a little one's cries are frequently met with anxiety, often born of the mothering person being unsure how to soothe this distress, the result can be what is called an *ambivalent* attachment for the child and *preoccupied* for the parent. The mother is lost in her own inner world part of the time, so she can't clearly see her infant's needs. Meanwhile, her baby experiences the mother's anxiety mixed with her genuine care, and this relational pattern begins to be wired into his or her brain. If this kind of caregiving continues, the child will begin to expect a feeling of chaos to come along with close relationships.

At the other end of the spectrum, if the mothering person has little access to emotion and is more comfortable in her left hemisphere, the crying infant will often look up into a bewildered or sometimes angry face that lacks resonance or understanding about the emotional needs of a little person with a just-developing brain. Because cognition is in the lead, it is very difficult for this mother to read the faces of others, so there can be little felt sense of her baby's needs. As a way of extending love, the parent may be able to meet all the expected external requirements—clean diapers and clothes, regular schedules—but more in a mechanical way than because she senses and responds to her baby's ever-changing flow of experience. This style of attachment is called *avoidant* for the baby and *dismissing* for the parent, because the parent is distant from the circuitry of warm connection, whereas the infant's right-hemisphere circuitry is seeking, seeking for a resonant and responding face, to no avail. If this kind of caregiving continues, the child will likely also become distant from his or her own emotions (except possibly anger) as a way to stay in contact with the parents by living up to their expectations (or by rebelling against them). Were this child able to feel it, there might be an inner sense of a profound emptiness instead of the warmth of security.

In some households, the chaos escalates toward abuse or the absence of emotion declines into coldness, hatred, and neglect. In both cases, responding to an infant's cries in an appropriate way is out of reach. Both of these lead to pockets of disorganized attachment, the painful fragmentation into terror that results from the baby having no possible strategy to stay in contact with her parent. Moving toward the parent draws the baby into the mother's terrifying fragmentation, and in moving away, the baby comes apart with no relational glue to hold him or her. For the baby this is a fearful experience without any hope of resolution (Main & Hesse, 1999). The parental style of attachment is called *unresolved* because it arises from unhealed traumas in the parents' early experience or from mental illness. In Chapters 3 and 4 we explored the disorganized attachment style that Bobby formed with his mother. Her own internal distress made it impossible for her to respond to Bobby's cries quickly and appropriately much of the time, and this lack of meeting between her CARE system and his PANIC/GRIEF calls left him with so much unresolved emotional pain.

This is just a brief and broad taste of the several flavors of attachment that can emerge, reflecting ways in which the inborn parental CARE system is filtered through the mothering person's own early childhood experience, influencing how she responds to her infant's PANIC/GRIEF cries. Panksepp's nested BrainMind hierarchy (Figure 3.4) can give us the sense of how the mother's cries brought a certain response from her parents that has now become part of the circular system between primary emotions and their secondary and tertiary manifestations in maternal behavior. Similarly, her responses to her own infant are encoding brain structures that will create a certain implicit pattern and flow of relationship—anticipations that can last a lifetime. These primary emotional experiences will then become nested in the secondary and tertiary levels of emotional processing in the baby's brain, leading to behaviors that further amplify the pattern. Fortunately, because of neuroplasticity, these patterns can change at any point in our lives. All the styles we have visited— from secure to ambivalent, avoidant, and disorganized—lie along a continuum, with each parent and child co-creating their own unique, unfolding dynamic pattern.

PLAYING, SEEKING, AND BONDING

In addition to the two systems we have just discussed (CARE and PANIC/GRIEF), Panksepp and Biven identify PLAY as one of three brain systems that generates nonsexual social bonds. Interactive play between infants and mothering people begins early, as we discussed in Chapter 2, and according to Panksepp and Biven, there is growing scientific evidence that primal PLAY urges, located in subcortical layers of the brain, are influential in the development of higher brain regions that foster happy, creative adult brains. In terms of brain chemistry, Panksepp (2009) tells us that the core of the PLAY system lies within the medial zones of the thalamus, in a particular area that is rich in opioids, along with the ascending dopamine systems that are so important for joy and laughter. He says, "It is a blessing that the urge for social play—for joyous physical engagement with others—was also not left to chance by evolution, but is built into the instinctual action apparatus of the mammalian brain" (p. 16).

This brings us back to Panksepp's nested BrainMind hierarchy (Figure 3.4) where we can see the importance of a joyous and playful environment in the early days of one's life because the patterns (or mental models) of these joyous activities will "nest" within the brain's top layers (the tertiary processing of the cortex), affecting cognitive development and relational capacity throughout the lifespan. This core PLAY system, coming from deeply subcortical areas of the brain, resides not only in the top layers but also in the middle layer, in the upper limbic areas where, according to Panksepp, secondary-process learning occurs. Here, we can literally develop an "emotional habit" of joyous connection. We will talk more about the importance of exuberant play as nested within the learning layers of the brain in Part III, where we will explore the vital role of the PLAY system in learning.

The SEEKING system, as substrate to all the other emotional systems, is one of the most continuously active instinctual emotional systems of the brain. In the context of attachment, this is the system that "allows animals to search for, find, and acquire all the resources that are needed for survival" (Panksepp & Biven, 2012, p. 95). We now know from the work of Bowlby and many neuroscientists who have studied attachment that infants require not only food, warmth, and shelter to survive, but also emotional connections with other human beings. Without these connections, infants do not thrive, and sometimes they even die in the absence of emotional support (Bowlby, 1953; Spitz & Wolf, 1946).

Even from the first day of life when infants reach out to their mothers with intense gazing, we can see their SEEKING systems coming online. Panksepp (2009) sometimes refers to this system as the *Desire System*, the system that mediates the appetitive desire that energizes each of us to engage with the world, not only for the resources we need to sustain ourselves physically, but also to fuel our search for meaning and social connections. In young children, we see this SEEKING system in high gear as they search for playmates and opportunities to engage in play. My grandson, after waiting patiently for me to finish some necessary tasks associated with his visit, will say, "Can we just play now?" So often PLAY and SEEKING are intertwined in the context of social attachments. What can be better for an infant or young child than to have playtime with the people who are closest to him or her, especially with mother, father, or a special grandparent?

PLAY: AN IMPORTANT BUILDING BLOCK OF ATTACHMENT

Allan Schore (2012) talks about the role of play episodes in developing a secure attachment between infants and caregivers. He describes the essential task of human infants for the first year of life as having two interrelated goals that arise within the relationship with the mothering person: (1) creation of a secure attachment bond of emotional communication and (2) development of the neural circuitry that gradually leads to greater capacity for self-regulation. As we said earlier, the infant SEEKING system is online the very first day of life. Infants reach out with their sensory capacities of smell, taste, touch, hearing, and vision to interact with their social environment. Then something quite noticeable takes place around 8 weeks of age. First-time mothers often experience their infants as somehow becoming "real" little persons at this age, capable of responding specifically to the mother's bids for relationship. Experienced mothers begin to anticipate this shift in their baby's behaviors somewhere between 6 to 8 weeks. They begin looking for the first smile and other signs of recognition and excitement in the baby that lets them know that this little person is ready for an interactive relationship. Schore (2012) explains:

> . . . by 8 weeks there is a dramatic progression of social and emotional capacities. Within episodes of mutual gaze, the mother and infant engage in intuitive and nonconscious facial, vocal, and gestural preverbal communications; and these highly arousing, affect-laden face-to-face interactions allow the infant to be exposed to high levels of social and cognitive information. The mother makes herself contingent, easily predictable, and manipulatable by the infant; and in order to regulate the high positive arousal, the dyad synchronizes the intensity of their affective behavior within lags of split seconds. (p. 228)

Let's linger over the words "contingent, easily predictable, and manipulatable by the infant." These joyous, playful dances have the potential of gradually expanding the baby's "window of tolerance" (Siegel, 1999), the degree of emotional intensity that he or she can hold without becoming disconnected and dysregulated. This expansion depends on the mother's own window of tolerance as well as her capacity for attunement with her infant. Often, when the mother hasn't experienced that kind of synchrony herself, her system has difficulty supporting micro-second, nonconscious attunement because the patterns simply aren't within her. Because of the speed with which they occur, they can't be manufactured by conscious decision. Many of the young ones who come to us for help may still be carrying the need for this kind of experience, so we have an opportunity in the playroom to be "contingent, easily predictable, and manipulatable" for the children who are with us because of early moments when they weren't met. In this way, as we work with specific issues with our young ones, we are also building the neural circuitry of secure attachment.

Schore (2012) continues: "These episodes of 'affect synchrony' occur in the first expression of social play and generate increasing levels of the positive affects of joy and excitement. In this interactive matrix both partners match states and then simultaneously adjust their social attention, stimulation, and accelerating arousal to each other's responses" (p. 228). We can recall the peek-a-boo play of Sammy and his dad (Chapter 2) as an example of how they used synchronous play to co-regulate one another. We saw how this kind of play helped develop Sammy's ANS as he and his father moved flexibly between states of hyper- and hypoarousal together. When Sammy signaled that he'd had enough, his father was able to read that signal and wait for Sammy to be ready to return to play. Their partnering in these joyous moments allowed Sammy's brain and nervous system to encode optimal ranges of play behavior (see Figure 2.1).

Ruth Newton and Allan Schore (Schore & Newton, 2012) explain the importance of these kinds of interactive play episodes from an interpersonal neurobiological perspective: They explain: "The mother's ability to down-regulate stressful high-arousal states through soothing and up-regulate stressful low-arousal states in play states acts as an epigenetic mechanism by which the connectivity between the central nervous (CNS) and autonomic nervous system (ANS) in the infant's developing emotional right brain is enhanced" (p. 387). She goes on to say that when the interactive regulation of stressful arousal (including the excitement of play) is optimal, it promotes the development of complex right-brain functions in the developing child, enhancing "affect regulation, attachment security, and a burgeoning positive sense of self" (p. 387).

From these early interactive social experiences, infants begin to understand how the world works. They learn whether or not it is a joyous and welcoming place, and whether they can expect others to help them when they are in need. By the time they are 12 months old, they have constructed, primarily in the nonverbal right hemisphere, a model of how it all works. What parents and other caregivers do *really matters*, and it matters for the entire lifespan. It matters because we carry these "internal working models" (Bowlby, 1969), or templates of how the world works, with us as a backdrop to our lives. Let's look at these models more closely keeping in mind our focus on why play matters.

MENTAL MODELS AND IMPLICIT MEMORIES

Through our early interactive social experiences with the people who are closest to us, we form what Bowlby (1969) aptly termed *internal working models* of the social world. Within the short span of the first 6 months of life, even before we can talk or develop specific styles of attachment with our caregivers, we learn the biological patterned sequences of social interactions that will become our models. Stern (1977/2002) gives us a beautiful description of what one of these social interactions looks like with a mother who is bottle-feeding her 3-month-old boy. During the first half of the feeding, the baby is intent on sucking, at times looking at his mother, and at other times, just looking around the room. The mother is generally still, although she glances at her baby periodically without talking to him or changing the expression on her face. The baby is intent on feeding, and the mother is careful not to distract him. And then a change begins to take place. The baby, while gazing at the ceiling, catches his mother's head turn toward him to gaze at him. He returns the gaze breaking the rhythm of his sucking. Stern (1977/2007) describes the play episode that followed:

> He let go of the nipple and the suction around it broke as he eased into the faintest suggestion of a smile. The mother abruptly stopped talking (to me) and, as she watched his face begin to transform, her eyes opened a little wider and her eyebrows raised a bit. His eyes locked on to hers, and together they held motionless for an instant. The infant did not return to sucking and his mother held frozen her slight expression of anticipation. This silent and almost motionless instant continued to hang until the mother suddenly shattered it by saying "Hey!" and simultaneously opening her eyes wider, raising her eyebrows further, and throwing her head up and toward the infant. Almost simultaneously, the baby's eyes widened. His head tilted up and, as his smile broadened, the nipple fell out of his mouth. Now she said, "Well hello! . . . heello . . . heeelloooo!", so that her pitch rose and the "hellos" became longer and more stressed on each successive repetition. With each phrase the baby expressed more pleasure, and his body resonated almost like a balloon being pumped up, filling a little more with each breath. The mother then paused and her face relaxed. They watched each other expectantly for a moment. The shared excitement between them ebbed, but before it faded completely, the baby suddenly took an initiative and intervened to rescue it. His head lurched forward, his hands jerked

up, and a fuller smile blossomed. His mother was jolted into motion. She moved forward, mouth open and eyes alight, and said, "Oooooh . . . ya wanna play do ya . . . yeah? . . . I didn't know if you were still hungry . . . no . . . nooooo . . . no I didn't. . . . " And off they went. (pp. 18–19)

What followed was about 4 minutes of interactive play between baby and mother, the excitement between them rising and falling in waves until the baby cued the mother that he'd had enough. The mother picked up on his cue immediately and helped him resume his feeding. In this brief play episode, we can see that this infant has already developed a lot of information about his mother's specific face, voice, touch, and movements. Stern (1977/2007) elaborates:

He has acquired schemas of the various changes they undergo to form different human emotional expressions and signals. He has "got" the temporal patterning of human behavior and the meaning of different changes and variations in tempo and rhythm. He has learned the social cues and conventions that are mutually effective in initiating, maintaining, terminating, and avoiding interactions with his mother. He has learned different discursive or dialogic modes, such as turn taking. And he now has the foundation of some internal composite picture of his mother so that, a few months after this phase is over, we can speak of his having established object permanence—or an enduring representation of mother that he carries around with him with or without her presence. (pp. 21–22)

If this little one continues to experience these interactive and attuned communication sequences as he grows up, his brain will be able to generalize across all these experiences, and he will develop a mental model that will become a strong foundation for his social–emotional relationships. They will guide him in his choice of key partnerships and also influence his level of resilience in stressful times.

In contrast, we can imagine in our examples of Alice (Chapter 2) and Bobby (Chapter 3) that these highly attuned play episodes were infrequent during early infancy. In an understaffed and overcrowded orphanage, it was unlikely that Alice had the spontaneous bouts of play that Stern describes when mother-infant relationships go well.

And although Bobby's father knew that his early life had been less than optimal, he could not comprehend how Bobby would have remembered the negative experiences since he was so young. Like many parents, what Bobby's father did not know is that these internal working models are stored in an implicit form in our brains and bodies. Although we don't "remember" implicit memories in the same way that we remember explicit memories, they powerfully influence our behaviors on a moment-to-moment basis because of the core patterns they hold.

HOW WE REMEMBER

If we look closely at how implicit and explicit memories are formed in the brain, we can begin to understand what might be happening when children like Bobby misbehave, or become highly anxious as Alice did when she was unable to speak at school. When Bobby's father asked why his son could not "remember" to behave, he, like many parents, probably believed that Bobby should be able to retrieve his father's verbal directive "to behave" from a memory storage system in his brain, like some sort of filing cabinet. And further, he expected that when Bobby found the correct file, he would be able to reproduce exactly what his father had said (and meant), like a photocopy of the words, "I want you to behave."

Unfortunately (and also fortunately!) the formation of memories in the brain is not so simple. Remembering is actually about the brain's ability to encode, store, and retrieve neural net profiles that are made up of the many associations of the events that we experience in our environments. As Daniel Siegel (2012) says, our brains are "experience dependent," linking past, present, and future together in dynamic and ever-changing neural nets of associated experiences. The once familiar concept of memories being stable like mountains is no longer relevant in the light of current neuroscience research. Donald Hebb's (1949) insight, which we can paraphrase as "neurons that fire together wire together," provides a picture of the current research-based concept that all aspects of an experience tend to gather into a neural net profile, encoding a representation of an entire event. For example, if our grandmother frequently baked chocolate chip cookies when she knew we were coming to visit, upon arrival, we would have been greeted by her welcoming voice, the wonderful smell of melted chocolate in the cookies, her smile, a warm hug, and perhaps the anticipation of sitting in her lap while she read our favorite story. Years later, just the smell of fresh baked cookies is enough to reawaken the memories, either with a wash of warm feelings through our bodies without being aware of the context or with both the full implicit and explicit memories of being with grandmother.

Likewise, when Bobby heard his exasperated father say, "Remember, I want you to behave today," his brain probably retrieved neural nets of multiple dysregulated comments from his abusive mother, his angry father, and his frustrated teachers. As he retrieved these neural nets from the past, he would have linked them to the present moment of hearing his father's words, responding to his tone of voice, seeing his angry face, and feeling the overly firm grip of his father's hand on his shoulder along with his own internal feelings of shame and unexpressed rage. Bobby would have encoded this experience and then stored it as a newly revised neural net of associations. As we accumulate experiences like these into larger nets, the probability for such neural nets to fire in the future increases. Eventually, with repetition, they become the mental models that drive our behavior at both cortical and subcortical levels.

We can understand these early memories more clearly by looking at the differences in the two major ways the brain makes memories. Figure 5.1 shows the hierarchical nature of the amygdala-centered implicit memories (bottom level) and the explicit memories (middle and top levels) that require hippocampal functioning. We are using a broken line between the types to indicate that there is a dynamic flow and potential integration among the levels.

Implicit Memories

In the first 12–18 months of life, before the hippocampus is fully developed and connected to the amygdala, researchers generally believe that we encode only at the implicit level (Ledoux, 1996; Schore, 2012). This is the embodied aspect of our experience that is part of every memory throughout our lives. Conscious attention is not required for encoding implicit memories, and when these memories are activated, we have no internal sensation of actually recall-

AUTOBIOGRAPHICAL EXPLICIT MEMORY

- Develops around 24 months and beyond
- Not solid until 4–5 years
- Requires conscious attention to encode
- Adds a sense of self & time to the story; e.g., "I was excited when I rode on the train yesterday."
- Involves the hippocampus and the prefrontal cortex
- When retrieved, there is a sense of recalling a series of episodic events that can be compared over time

EXPLICIT MEMORY

- Develops between 12 to 18 months
- Not solid until 4–5 years
- Hippocampus links required
  - LH with facts
  - RH with self-related episodic memory
- Requires conscious attention to encode
- When retrieved, there is a sense of recollection
- Adds time element; past tense becomes possible
- Includes semantic (factual) and episodic (self across time) memory

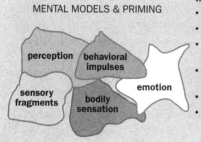

IMPLICIT MEMORY

- Pre-birth to 12–18 months (Implicit Only)*
- Amygdala centered
- Does not require conscious attention to encode
- Includes behavioral impulses, emotions, perceptions, bodily sensations and images
- No time stamp
- When retrieved, it lacks internal sensation of being recalled

*We are always making implicit memories.

FIGURE 5.1. Levels of Memory. Adapted from Badenoch (2008), Siegel and Hartzell (2003), and Siegel (2010).

ing anything. For example, when we are driving an automobile, we automatically coordinate a number of complicated tasks—steering, accelerating, and braking—all simultaneously without having to think much about the complexity of these highly integrated and interwoven skills, and no sensation that we are remembering them from previous experiences. This example of implicit memory is also called *procedural memory*, and it is the kind of memory that we use to learn new skills.

Another kind of implicit memory is encoded when we are in relational situations—such as early attachment relationships. If my mother had frequent angry episodes when I was small, the implicit memory of this experience may include a tight belly, an attempt to move away, a feeling of fear, and a sense that the world of relationships is unsafe. I might also encode fragments such as the look in her eyes, the sound of her voice, or the way the light is shining through the window. Many years later, in the presence of anger (or when the light is at a certain angle), this neural net may awaken and flood my body with all of these fragments from the past, but with no sense that I am remembering. Instead, it will seem that this full array of experiences is arising from the current incident, even though the response may seem to be out of proportion. In this way, the past is always with us.

Implicit memories create an ongoing undercurrent influencing our moment-to-moment experience. They are with us in the form of bodily sensations (a warmth in the chest or a tightening in the belly), waves of feeling (joy or fear), behavioral impulses (if we feel safe, an impulse to open and move toward; if we feel unsafe, an impulse to protect), perceptual shifts (a filter "coloring" the tone of the present experience with the past), and sometimes sensory fragments (the smell of chocolate chip cookies or shampoo). This undercurrent of implicit memories carries the entire range of our life experiences, from positive to negative, into the felt experience of the present— meaning, they sometimes enhance our current functioning, but can as well create havoc as we will see when we begin to address treatment issues in Parts II and III.

One of the challenging (and also beneficial) aspects of implicit memories is their lack of a timestamp. Badenoch (2011) notes, "They reside out of the usual flow of time that gives us a sense of memories slipping into the past" (p. 28). If the memories are of warm and nurturing relationships, it can be beneficial to have these fully available as if "present" when we are with others. They will have a tendency to bias the interaction in the direction of a good outcome because that's what we anticipate. Our behaviors, then, will match this expectation. If, however, negative or painful implicit memories are activated, we can have a profound perceptual shift that tells us that the same thing is happening again, regardless of what may be unfolding in the present moment. Our behavioral impulse will be guided by this felt sense, and that behavior can bring on something similar to what happened in the past. For example, if I have seen my father's frowning face many times and felt his anger, and these experiences have not been witnessed and comforted, any frowning face, whether it is directed at me or not, can awaken the felt sense of shame. As I duck my head to avoid criticism or become defensive, the other person's response may follow my lead, resulting in the very rupture in relationship I was fearing. We often see these kinds of entanglements in cases of trauma or attachment loss (more about this topic in Part II).

Siegel (2010) describes these domains of implicit memory as the "puzzle pieces of the mind that form the foundation for how the past continues to influence us in the present" (p. 150). Our brain gathers experience into associated networks, and it continually draws on these implicit elements from the past to get us ready for dealing with the future. These expectations of our unfolding lives become the mental models that drive our behaviors and life decisions.

Recall Stern's (1977/2002) example of the baby boy and his mother playing briefly during a bottle-feeding. We can see in this example one behavioral sequence (or play episode) that was filled with pleasure. Panksepp's (Panksepp & Biven, 2012) primary-process emotional systems of CARE and PLAY came together to create an experience of joyful connection. If these play episodes are repeated frequently, the infant comes to form expectations about the way the social world works. Remembering that neurons that fire together wire together, we can see how this baby boy begins to form neural networks holding all aspects of these positive social interactions. These implicit memories also create what is called *priming*, which helps the brain get ready to respond in certain ways. This baby learns to anticipate that relationships with others may be joyful. His little face, filled with this expectation, has a good chance of provoking a delighted response from others.

Conversely, mental models and priming can also lead to the expectation of negative outcomes. Our 9-year-old Bobby seems to be primed, more often than not, for the disappointment of failed connections. From his early implicit memories, gathered into neural nets of negative interpersonal experiences, Bobby's brain begins to generalize how relationships usually go. As he moves into relationship with anyone, his body tenses in preparation for disappointment, fear, and pain, sometimes followed by activation of his RAGE system. As his behavioral impulse is shaped by this unfolding experience, he draws further anger and punishment from those around him, deepening and strengthening this embodied anticipation. However, thanks to our brain's ongoing availability to change even implicit memories, it was possible for Dr. Matthews to relate to Bobby in a way that could shift his anticipations.

Explicit Memories

Between 12 and 18 months, with the development of the hippocampus and its connection to the amygdala, explicit memories begin to form, although the capacity for generating a more steady stream of explicit memories usually takes until we are 4 or 5 years old. Siegel (2010) calls the hippocampus the "master puzzle piece assembler" as it helps to bring the various elements of implicit memory into a single picture or story with a beginning, middle, and end. For the first time, there can be a sense of past and future. Explicit memories require conscious attention to encode, so we make fewer of them than implicit memories.

Explicit memories include semantic (factual) and episodic (the sense of self across time, which includes autobiographical) memories. When we are having explicit memories, unlike when we are having implicit memories, we have a sense that we are actually remembering something. When I tell a story of how my father played hide-and-seek with my brothers and sisters and me, I am recalling a specific explicit memory. I know that I was around 4 or 5 years of age, and I know it was inside our home in the small town of Springboro, Pennsylvania. Integrated with this explicit memory are the implicit elements: the excitement (bodily sensation) and joy (feeling) of playing together, the pretend stalking and pouncing (behavioral impulses), the smell of the popcorn (sensory fragment), along with the felt sense of the goodness of families doing things together just for fun (perception). Now when my grandson comes to my home and initiates a game of hide-and-seek, I may not have the sense that I am recalling the implicit part of this childhood experience, but all aspects of these implicit memories support the way my body moves naturally into play with him.

At the top level of Figure 4.1 we see autobiographical explicit memory, which begins to develop around the age of 2. When we retrieve autobiographical memories, we have a sense of recalling a series of episodic events that can be compared over time, a narrative of our experience. By adding the sense of ourselves, this kind of explicit remembering allows us to make sense of our life stories. With this capacity, we are able to verbalize how we experience an event in the context of time. For example, we can say, "I was excited when I rode the train yesterday," or "I felt mad when Julia took my ball." This kind of remembering can be an invitation to those close to us to hold our experience with us, to listen without judgment while we integrate what we have experienced into the developing narrative of our lives. We will return to this form of memory in Chapters 9 and 10 where we talk about the storytelling brain and how play so easily activates it.

Memories and the Hierarchical Brain

We placed implicit memories at the bottom of the chart to denote not only how early they appear in our development, but also to show them as foundational to the rest. This hierarchical nature of the levels of memory may provide a bridge to understanding the role of play in emotional and cognitive development. As we saw in the work of Perry and Panksepp in Chapter 3, the hierarchical levels of brain processing, including now the levels of memory, give us a template for understanding why early experiences are so important. This template is also important as we move into clinical contexts where healing comes to the fore. If we are willing to collaborate with the inherent structure of the mind–brain as Mother Nature crafted it, our task of formulating interventions becomes much easier.

THE PLAYING MOTHER

I want to conclude this chapter with the wonderful image of "The Playing Mother," given to us by Daniel Stern (1977/2002). He suggests that an infant's repeated experiences with an attuned and playful mother, across a number of different contexts, may actually be instrumental to his or her ability to form a representation of the mother. Highly attuned mothers play frequently with their infants regardless of context or whatever task is at hand. During bath time, this mother echoes the baby's rhythmic splashing of the rubber ducky in the water with her smiles, her energized vocalizations, and the splashing of her own hand in the water. During feeding, she plays airplane with a circling spoonful of food to get the baby's attention, helping him or her to refocus on eating. Even during unpleasant diapering, the mother might say in a lilting, rhythmical, and excited voice, "You are my very best stinky little boy/girl," while giving him an affectionate tickle on his tummy. If you ask mothers why they play with infants, most of them will have no other answer than, "It's just fun." It seems so intuitive and so very natural.

If you study mother–infant play, however, you start to see a much more complex picture. Stern (1977/2002) helps us to understand how these frequently recurring play episodes help infants established object permanence—that consolidated representation of the mother that infants retain whether or not Mommy is present. This happens around 9 months of age, when we see the developmental landmarks of stranger anxiety, separation reactions, and then reunion responses. At that point, we know that the infant is beginning to consolidate an internal representation of the mother. How does this happen?

Prior to the development of stranger anxiety and before the baby develops a preference for a primary caretaker, there have been an incredible number of mother–infant interactions. From Panksepp's (Panksepp & Biven, 2012) perspective, we know that these interactions have involved many PLAY episodes intertwined with the CARE, SEEKING, and PANIC/GRIEF systems. These mother–infant *interactions*, however, are not the same as a mother–infant *relationship*. How does the infant make a transition from the composites of interactions to the relationship state?

Stern (1977/2002) says that this is a "difficult leap," because the relationship state entails more than the sum of all the past and present interactions. He explains:

> Conceptually it is a different kind of organization, or a different integration of experience. One of its central features is an enduring mental image, or schema, or representation of the other person. In most psychological theories, beginning with psychoanalysis, this enduring internal representation is the sine qua non of object permanence. (p. 117)

Stern further notes that the "representation of persons" requires three elements: (1) an infant acting upon an object (objects include human beings), (2) the infant receiving a sensory experience (a response stimulated by his or her action upon the object), and (3) the infant having an excitatory affective experience. The first two elements are known as sensory–motor action schemas whereby infants develop mental schemas. For example, they learn what a rattle is after repeated experiences of acting upon and receiving stimuli from a class of objects known as rattles. These mental schemas, however, are not the same as the internal representation of another person. How does the third element emerge?

As with the sensory–motor units of experience, these interactive units of human relationship (now containing the affective element) must be practiced over and over again if the infant is to internalize them into a representation of another person. How does this happen? Stern suggests that affective play sequences may be instrumental in helping the baby to practice these basic sensory–motor–affective experience units with the mother. Stern (1977/2002) explains:

> Once the infant has formed even a moderately comprehensive representation, he can be said to bring to each new interactive event a history of the relationship, in the form of the representation. This "history" then affects the course of each new interaction. Similarly, the sensory–motor–affective experience of each new interaction, once internalized, may alter the configuration of the history as it progresses. A dynamic interaction thus evolves between the past and the present, between established representations and current exchanges, between the relationship and the ongoing interaction. Conceived in this fashion, it is quite understandable that each infant–caregiver pair can

develop an individual course for their own relationship, and that the outcome of seemingly similar interactions can be quite divergent for different pairs with different histories. Relationships thus take on direction and momentum. (p. 130)

Stern (1977/2002) then paints a picture for us of how mother and baby manage these sensory–motor–affective experiential units over time. In their varied activities, including feeding, diapering, bathing, and so on, play activities seem to have a way of spontaneously emerging no matter what the context. So although the baby may have varied experiences of the "feeding mother," the "bathing mother," and the "diapering mother," it is the "playing mother" that consistently reappears. Stern says, "In this way, the constant reappearance of the 'playing mother' . . . may help to facilitate the infant's integration of a fully consolidated representation" (p. 132).

Play is core to our deep social relationships. We play with our infants. We become part of them, and they become part of us.

PART II

Playing with the Brain in Mind

Chapter 6

BRIDGING THEORIES OF PLAY AND PRACTICAL APPLICATIONS

Using the first part of this book as a foundation, we turn now to the practical aspects of using play for healing purposes with both children and adults. In making this transition from theory to practice, we will keep in mind how the system of PLAY and playful activities can be used as processes for creating joyful, resilient, and productive lives. We will explore the many ways we can collaborate with the natural dynamic flow of brains and minds (Siegel, 2012) as they move from simplicity to complexity, staying alert to moments and sequences of differentiating and integrating play. We will continue to draw from Panksepp's (Panksepp and Biven, 2012) core emotional systems and Porges's (2011) polyvagal definition of play. Thinking about the rhythmical and relational needs of our patients from the perspective of Perry's (2009) neurosequential model will help us to stay grounded in the practical realities of our moment-by-moment decisions in our brain-building interventions. Our knowledge of the pleasurable communication template that is built from early dyadic play experiences (Stern, 1977/2002) will guide us in our relational play activities. We also will take direction from modern attachment theory (Schore, 2012) to explore how healing and therapeutic practice emerge from our core biological and psychological needs to connect with others, and how our warm presence and micro-second responsiveness can build the neural circuitry of attachment that will last a lifetime.

Drawing from the principles of interpersonal neurobiology that we have been learning in Part I, let's explore how we can move into practical realities, while keeping in mind the following guidelines:

1. Neuroception of safety (Porges): Our nervous system needs to detect safety in the environment for us to use our social engagement systems effectively.

2. Motivational system of PLAY (Panksepp): The urge to play is an ancestral tool inherited at birth for developing a joyous, creative, and relational rich life.

3. Hierarchical nature of the brain (Perry, Panksepp, and Siegel): Bottom-up processing (rhythmic patterns, sensory experiences, bodily based action patterns, primary emotional systems) and top-down processing (cognitive processing, mental recognition) are integral to one another.

4. Application of complexity theory in living systems, including brain–mind systems (Siegel): There is a natural movement from simplicity to complexity in the brain's push toward wholeness.

5. Pathways of integration (Siegel): There are numerous pathways along which the brain–mind achieves integration (a state of mental health).

6. The interwoven nature of the PLAY system with CARE, SEEKING, and PANIC/GRIEF (Panksepp): Play is a core element of attachment because it provides ample opportunities for the attunement that is necessary in developing emotional regulation and the anticipation of positive relationships.

7. Implicit memories of dyadic play in attachment (Schore and Stern): Positive dyadic play creates a life-long template for emotional regulation so that our social relationships can blossom.

Our goal in Part II is to condense and translate into play therapy language some of the main concepts of interpersonal neurobiology that are flowing out of several decades of burgeoning neuroscience studies. It is both exciting and daunting to know how to incorporate what we are rapidly learning from current neuroscience into the everyday practices of play therapy. Within the therapeutic hour, there is a constant need to weave together, in a dynamic way, the art of our clinical interventions with the most current scientific concepts available. Research about the developing brain and mind enables us to collaborate more effectively at a practical level with each unique person who comes into our play therapy offices. We can have sophisticated theoretical models, hundreds of therapeutic tools at our disposal, and state-of-the-art playrooms, but only when we collaborate with the developing mind will we be as effective as we want to be.

Let's begin this journey of translation and collaboration by asking how we can best use these concepts to guide our ways of being present and our moment-by-moment decisions in the play therapy environments. How do we talk to parents, teachers, and other concerned colleagues about how play relationships affect the structure and functioning of brains and minds? Most challenging, how can we say it so simply and so accurately that even our children can begin to comprehend this amazing organ of adaptation that we all have and share with one another?

Chapter 7

PLAY SANCTUARIES

At the stage reached by the age of three, and after ages
four, five, six, play will be necessary. These are games
which nature herself suggests at that age; children readily invent these for themselves when left in one another's company. All children of the specified ages, that of
three to six, should first be collected at the local sanctuary—all the children of each village being thus assem-
bled at the same place. Further, the nurses are to have
an eye to the decorum or indecorum of their behavior.

—Plato, *The Laws*, VII, 794

In several different writings, Panksepp quotes Plato (above) to direct
our attention to the long-held idea that play is essential in children's
development. Panksepp believes that society would do well to follow
Plato's advice and invest in creating "play sanctuaries"—places where
children are safe to invent their own creative play activities (Panksepp, 2007; Panksepp & Biven, 2012). He thinks it would help restore
something that many of our children have lost in the modern world
—opportunities for abundant play.

Plato's play sanctuary is a physical space set aside for play—a
place of refuge and protection from reality. Like bird sanctuaries,
sanctuaries of worship, or wildlife sanctuaries, these are physical
spaces that we set aside for special use. We can enter these spaces

with the freedom of knowing that we can pursue a special need without fear of intruders, criticism, or predators. Although we usually think of sanctuaries as physical spaces, they also can be emotional or psychological spaces. Play is a good example. Fred Rogers, child development specialist, seemed to understand this concept when he said, "Play allows us a safe distance as we work on what's close to our hearts" (Rogers, 1994, p. 59).

When we enter into this kind of play, we are going into an internal sanctuary, where we know that no matter how silly we act or how goofy we might look to others, we are safe from criticism (from others and from self) because we are "just playing." We can say to ourselves (or others), "I didn't really mean it." Or "Just kidding! I was pretending." Somehow we allow ourselves to step into this psychological play space where we are fully acceptable just as we are.

FREEDOM, PROTECTION, AND SANCTUARY

Play sanctuaries simultaneously provide freedom and protection. The boundary where protection begins, whether visible or invisible, is a condition for freedom. The protected boundaries set a limit, physically or psychologically, to free us to be who we really are. Dora Kalff (1980, 2003), originator of a Jungian-based version of sand tray therapy, said that one of the primary tasks of the play therapist is to create a "free and protected space" for emotional healing. She described her play space as invitational, with a variety of materials (paints, clay, mosaics, plaster of Paris, sand trays, miniature figurines, and other things) that would engage the child's imagination. Sandplay was her specialty, and so she used it as an example to talk about how this particular modality offered both the freedom and protection necessary for healing:

> The child has absolute freedom in determining what to construct, which figures to choose and how to use them. The same limitations that are prerequisite for genuine freedom in the real world are present in the measurements of the sandbox. They are scaled down to one-person size, thereby forming limits to what can be represented in providing a frame wherein transformation can take place. Quite unconsciously, the child

experiences, what I call a free, and at the same time, protected space. (Kalff, 2003, p. 17)

Kalff then discussed 9-year-old Christopher, who was frequently truant from school and highly anxious. As she talked about his play therapy, she revealed her deep understanding that the "free and protected" space is not just in the construction of the physical space. It also is held within the "being of the therapist" in the way she composes herself when she is with her patients. At one point in Christopher's therapy, Kalff related that he reconstructed a broken locomotive, made tracks for it, and then designed several switches for it. They sat on the floor together while he taught her how to maneuver the train through the switches. Kalff said, "I let him direct me. If I forgot something, such as throwing a switch, it gave him the chance to correct me. He became my teacher in this game and thus grew into a new role. Here, he knew something that I still had to learn!" (p. 28).

On the floor of the playroom, Kalff showed us how she used herself, as a person, to contain Christopher's anxiety. She allowed him to grow into a new role by making room for him to become an active agent in teaching her something that she really did not know. In this sense, the "therapist herself" becomes the sanctuary, or as we sometimes say, the therapist is the container for whatever psychological difficulties the patient brings. We will say more about how the therapist does this at a practical level when we talk about mindfulness and the relational nature of play therapy.

INVITATION TO PLAY

Most children don't need formal invitations to play. Their combined PLAY and SEEKING circuits seem to be perpetually turned on, and as many play scholars have suggested, it is a good thing. Without the curiosity of the SEEKING system and the experimenting of the PLAY system, children might never learn all the things they need to know before they enter the adult world. Children are usually good, however, at finding ways to interject play whenever they can and wherever they are. So although they don't need special playrooms to invite their play behaviors into action, a special environment designed specifically with the PLAY circuitry in mind is a hard one to pass up. Even for many adults, it is hard not to at least feel a pull toward active play when the environment says, "This is a good place to play."

Play Spaces for Children

Since new information enters the brain through the sensory system, and since most children are still absorbing the world kinesthetically, it is important to provide play therapy props that will engage their senses and quickly attract their SEEKING and PLAY systems, helping to open the motivational brain circuitry and anchor the therapy.

What kind of props do children need, and how do we choose them? Keeping our guidelines in mind (Chapter 6), let's begin with the hierarchical nature of the brain. From Bruce Perry's (2006, 2009) neurosequential model and Panksepp's (2011) nested hierarchy, we know that the early development of the brain stem is critical for the emotional regulation that is at the heart of psychotherapy and child development. Perry reminds us again and again how important the repetitive patterning of the brain stem is. He reminds us that the infant's intrauterine experiences are about rhythm to a great extent. The infant is comforted by the mother's heartbeat after birth, and the mother's rhythmic patterns of interaction play a major role in providing the patterned, repetitive sensory stimulation and experiences that help organize the child's developing brain. For children with histories of early neglect and abuse, repetitive rhythmic sequences are especially important, but none of us is exempt from the powerful influences of repetitive and rhythmical sensory stimulation.

Based on this brain concept (our body's need for rhythmical regulation), play props that provide this kind of sensory input are important. We can include a few musical instruments, especially drums. Balls are helpful toys, too, especially good for rhythmic turn taking. We can throw Nerf balls in most any environment, and bouncing balls are a good addition if the room allows for it. One toy that recently found its way to the market place is the Hoberman sphere, or what I call the *breathing ball*. It is colorful, it expands and contracts, and it can easily be manipulated to synchronize with the rhythm of our breathing.

A rocking chair (child- or adult-sized) is a great addition to any play space, along with chairs that swivel. We can include visual rhythmic objects also. In my sand tray miniature collection, I have small figurines that move and can be manipulated by most any child or adult for a visual rhythmical experience. Consider adding yo-yos, sand pendulums (from Wind&Weather.com), balance mobiles (OfficePlayground.com), and anything that moves in a rhythmical way.

Transitional Play Objects

So often children ask, "May I take this home?" Or sometimes, when we are not watching, they simply slip an object into their pockets. Very young children do not necessarily know about "stealing," and we could have a discussion about that, but for now let's consider how children use transitional objects to build internal safety. Infants and young children use external objects to help them internalize the presence of Mother, whether she is physically with them or not. My daughter had her transitional blanket, and I still remember (40 years later) having to make a trip back to the babysitter's house to retrieve the forgotten blanket.

The brain is an associational organ, and if an infant is touching the silky, smooth feeling of the binding on her blanket at the same time that her mother is singing a lullaby while rocking her to sleep, it is highly likely that the sensations of the blanket binding will become associated in the infant's brain with the mother's soothing behaviors. When the infant touches the binding again (whether the mother is present or not), the sensation will reawaken the memory of mother's comfort (remember, "neurons that fire together, wire together"), and she will apparently soothe herself (although she is actually coming back into relationship with her internalized mother). We call this *self-regulation*, and I believe that children sometimes use playroom objects in a similar way. The presence of the nonjudgmental therapist is soothing and healing, and an object can easily become associated with this soothing at the same time as our young ones are internalizing us.

One possibility for dealing with the request to take a toy home is to have a "borrowing box" of small items that a child can take home with the understanding that once it is returned, he or she can then borrow another object. Another way to deal with this issue is to have a basket or small container of some kind that serves as a child's "special cubby" in the playroom where he or she can keep something safe until returning for the next session. I once treated a 7-year-old Russian girl who had been adopted from an orphanage. For some period of time, she checked every week when she first came into the playroom to make sure that the little boat she had used in her sand tray (and selected for special keeping) was still in her personal basket.

We cannot always let a child remove things from the community collection to take home or to store away in his or her private cubby because then other children do not have access to that particular object. But in rare circumstances, it is sometimes worth the extra management to accommodate this need. In the case of the 7-year-old adopted child, I transferred the little boat back and forth from the community collection to her basket until she was finished with the safekeeping of the object. I did that only because there was another child who also used that item regularly in his play.

An easier way to manage this problem is to say, "This _____ [particular object] has to stay here in the playroom, but we can take a picture of it, and you can take the picture home (or put it in your cubby)." On that note, I think it is really important *not* to say to a child that the object has to stay in the playroom because other children need to play with it. It is too hard for some of them to even think about sharing with another child a particular object that has become precious. I am sure that my daughter could not easily have shared her transitional blanket with another toddler. It is also hard for many of our child patients to have to think about other children coming into the playroom for special time with us. There is a place to teach sharing, but it is certainly not the first task of play therapy. Generally it is more productive to preserve the sanctity of the special child–therapist relationship.

Special Play Areas in the Play Therapy Office

Keeping in mind the many different types of play and the wide range of needs and learning styles that children bring into the playroom, it is useful to set up special areas for costumes, art, games, and sandplay to meet a variety of children's needs. Providing these diverse areas also allows children to self-regulate their ANSs by being able to move from one area to another when symbolic play gets too close to the reality of their painful experiences.

Molly, an 8-year-old girl with encopresis,[1] is a good example of how children instinctively use movement from one play area to another to protect the safety of their play. Molly created a beach scene in the sand tray with miniature figurines. As children so often do, she began telling a story as she manipulated the sand tray figures. She said, "The family took their dog and went to the beach for an overnight camping trip." As she talked, she set up the beach umbrellas and then spread out the food on the miniature tablecloth. She continued: "After they ate their dinner, they put their tents up and went to sleep. When they woke up in the morning, the dad discovered that he had been sleeping on dog poop. Yikes!" Molly stopped dead in her tracks. She was silent for about 10 seconds, and then she said, without looking at me, "Can we play Candyland now?"

Molly was encopretic only at home, and given her history of sexual abuse (by her uncle), she very likely experienced a great deal of shame at this point in the story, followed by a sudden drop in her dorsal vagal nervous system when she said the word *poop* out loud. Her father was often angry with her when she soiled herself. It is no wonder that she was so startled by her own storytelling when it got too close to the reality of her problem. What a relief for her to be able to choose Candyland, a well-structured game, providing lots of safety (and easy reconnection with me). It was a good way for her to recover. Molly was about 8 weeks into her therapy, and up to that point, she had been quite devoted to telling sand tray stories. For several weeks after the "poop story," she didn't touch the sand. She loved telling stories, however, and so she began to use the hand puppets to work with a variety of themes, including one story about a smelly skunk. After a period of time when Molly was able to reestablish safety, she resumed her play in the sand. Although she avoided telling stories about "poop" in the tray, she did tell stories about mothers who were horrified to see how dirty their children had become from playing in the mud. With the freedom to redirect herself, Molly simply found a safe way to continue her therapeutic play.

Organization and Predictability

Keeping the playroom organized can be a challenge, but it is especially important for patients who have been traumatized by the loss of control that is so often a part of the traumatic experience. Being able to find a specific object in a specific place offers predictability in a world that seems all too unpredictable. I once worked with an adult woman who was making sand trays regularly to deal with old wounds of severe childhood physical and sexual abuse. Without exception, she would begin her sand tray building process by going to the shelves to find a very small and very specific white owl. That little owl was in every sand tray that she built, and it seemed to anchor and connect her trays over time. She never named the object as an owl, nor did she ever say what it meant to her, but I could sense her relief every time she reached for it and placed it in her world. This patient needed me to keep the playroom organized so that she could find the object that was precious to her consistently in its place.

Cleanup issues seem like a mundane topic in the context of the interpersonal neurobiology of play. Nonetheless, how we handle cleanup can serve as an important opportunity to communicate to a child that the playroom is a special place where normal expectations of being neat and orderly do not necessarily hold. Allowing a child to leave the play space without cleaning up helps to establish a permissiveness that is helpful in creating an emotional neuroception of safety. It communicates to the child that what he or she does and says (or doesn't do and say) in the playroom is acceptable.

This value of permissiveness in the playroom can be very difficult for some parents, and I think it is important to discuss with them the interpersonal implications. When indicated, I try to address their fears that the permissiveness of the playroom will spoil their children, and I assure them that it is also okay to have rules at home for cleanup and organization. When I introduce the child to the playroom (usually with the parent present), I might say something like this:

"This is a special playroom, and in here you can do anything you like, and if there is something that you can't do, I will let you know. In here

we don't have to clean up when we are finished playing. It's only here though, because I know you still have cleanup rules at home."

When I talk with parents about the permissiveness in the playroom, I try to make sure that they understand that I am *not* giving their child license to misbehave.

Privacy for the Play Therapy Room

How do we communicate to children that the playroom is a safe place in which they can explore the painful areas of their lives? Children are often sensitive to the nonverbal cues from parents, teachers, or peers about whether or not it is okay to play in a certain way. Since we are trying to provide the neuroception of safety (Porges, 2011), we need to make sure that our patients can share their deepest pain without fear of being judged. Ideally we want to provide a physical environment that ensures privacy (from peering eyes or attempts to overhear). If soundproofing isn't possible, having a little distance between the waiting area and the play area helps. If even this option isn't possible, placing a sound machine just outside the door is useful.

Play Spaces for Adults

Most of the things we have said about creating play spaces for children apply to adults as well. Adults can benefit from many of the same play activities as children do, such as art, clay, and sand tray building. The aesthetic needs of adults should be taken into consideration, however, and the décor and organization of the play space should communicate, "This is a good place for adults to play." Otherwise, they may dismiss the usefulness of the play activities with a comment, "Oh, you work with children, too."

I work with both children and adults, and so I have tried to organize my playroom in a way that does not offend adults or restrict children's imaginations. I have noticed that children appreciate the aesthetic qualities of what I have created for my adult clients, and although it is somewhat more expensive to create a multipurpose playroom to serve both children and adults, it is less expensive than setting up two separate offices. I do have some objects in my sand tray collection that I do not make available to children. The reason I set them aside for adults only (in a shelf area that is too high for children, or in a closed cupboard) is that they are either too fragile for children or too difficult to clean up. For example, I have a small basket of amethyst gemstones and another of lavender seeds that I do not make available to children because if a child decides to dump the entire contents of the basket into the sand or onto the floor, the impending cleanup leaves me too anxious about getting ready for my next patient. Children know immediately when we are anxious. When we become dysregulated, they also become dysregulated (more on this later). The bottom line for me is to offer the widest range of play props that I can for the sake of increasing fun, creativity, and joy in my playroom without losing my calm and present state with those who come to play.

Flexible Boundaries within the Play Sanctuary

Conflicts are inevitable during sibling or family play or peer group play. Since I agree with Kalff (2003) that the therapist needs to make sure that patients have a free and protected space for play (internally and externally), I think of my playroom as having safe internal boundaries that are movable and flexible as needed. For example, two brothers (5 and 9 years old) were playing with soldiers in a sand tray during their joint play session, and of course "war" broke out. I stayed in my witnessing and reflective mode until the war turned personal and the complaints about each other increased a decibel or so. At that point, I said, "Oh, something really important is happening here. Neither of you likes having the guns of the other guys pointed at your guys. What shall we do?" The complaints became more bitter and ratcheted another decibel higher.

Realizing that the physical play area of the sand tray was no longer safe, I said even more emphatically, "Oh, this really *is* important. We need to do something about this. Okay, come over here (*motioning them to a spot about 4 feet away from the sand area*). Let's figure this out so you can keep playing." We temporarily created a conflict-solving area apart from the play area. In the next 5 minutes, I simply reflected each of their positions, while continuing to insist that they come up with a solution they both could accept. Without any advice from me, they were able to resolve the issue, and they resumed their play successfully. In a follow-up telephone call, the father told me that his older son said, on the way home, "That was really fun!" It was especially important for these two boys to resolve their differences in the play because their parents were involved in a high-conflict divorce with almost no skills to resolve their differences.

How I Feel in My Own Therapy Playroom

Over the years, I have created a number of different playrooms. My first play space, one that was assigned to me, was very small with no windows, few toys, and a large ugly gray steel desk that I despised. When I first walked in, I knew that it was going to be hard to live with the outdated orange carpet, the green lampshade, and the ugly steel desk. I never did convince the director of the agency to remove the desk, but I spent a weekend painting and refurbishing until I knew that my own creative spirit could feel playful and happy in the space. My budget was spare, but I used one small corner of the room to create a visually delightful play area. When I walked into the room, my eyes went to the play space instead of the ugly desk, and I could tell that my patients were delighted, too. Eventually, when I started my private practice, I rented a space with windows and a door to access an outside play area, and I furnished it just the way I wanted. It was aesthetically pleasing to me, and it nurtured my sense of creative playfulness and vitality.

In taking care of my own spirit of play and creativity, no matter how modest or elaborate the play space, I have always believed that my patients would know implicitly, "This is a good place to play." The valuable ongoing lesson for me from my first modest playroom is how important it is to respect the way we feel in our own dedicated play area. Play spaces grow from the inside out. Preserving my internal play sanctuary made it possible for me to imagine and then provide a physical space that did indeed become a play sanctuary for emotional healing.

CHAPTER NOTE

1. Encopresis is an elimination disorder that involves repeatedly having bowel movements in inappropriate places after the age when bowel control is normally expected. Encopresis is also called *soiling* or *fecal incontinence* (*Encyclopedia of Mental Disorders*, http://www.minddisorders .com).

Chapter 8

PLAYING TOGETHER: THE COLLABORATIVE RELATIONSHIP

Feeling safe in a relationship is so important when we have to deal with life's stressful events. As Jaak Panksepp says in the Foreword to Margot Sunderland's (2006) *The Science of Parenting*, "Children whose emotional feelings are cherished and respected, even their angry outbursts, shall live more happily than those whose early passions are denied" (p. 7). Four-year-old Eddie was up against an upsetting time. As an only child of adoring parents, he was thrown for a loop one day when his parents brought baby Kate home from the hospital. It was true that they had "prepared" him for this event by talking about his new baby sister and how exciting it would be when she came. However, nothing had "prepared" him for sharing his mother's lap or having less one-on-one time with his dad.

When baby Kate was about 3 weeks old, Eddie walked into my playroom and headed directly for the shelves of sand tray toys. He found a tiny baby wrapped in a pink blanket and put it in the center of the sand tray that was sitting in the middle of the playroom. He then went back to the shelf, picked up a small crocodile with movable jaws, and walked over to the tray. Swooping down to pick up the baby with the crocodile jaws, he kept on walking until he was about 4 feet away from the tray, where he released the baby from the jaws. She plummeted to the floor. Eddie put the crocodile back on the shelf. Without looking back at the baby or the crocodile, he turned to me and said, "Okay, let's play trains."

He got the toy train out of its case and asked me to help him construct the tracks. We played together with the train for a few minutes while he made whistling and chugging sounds, and then he explained to me how the train was going to go pick up logs that needed to be taken to the sawmill. Eddie never mentioned the tiny baby on the floor or the crocodile that was now safely back on the shelf. Nor did he share any news about his baby sister, Kate. Nor did I ask.

During his 1-minute sand tray, I didn't reflect with words what I witnessed with the baby and crocodile. Eddie and I simply held this eloquent play action within the silence of our safe and warm relationship. In retrospect, I can view this as a therapeutic decision to remain silent, although in the moment it was a split-second intuitive response to Eddie. At a cognitive level, I did not ask myself if I should respond immediately with words, or if I should bring it up later in the session. Nor did it occur to me that I might need to check with the parents to see if Eddie was expressing any aggression toward his baby sister. It just felt like the right thing to do—to hold Eddie's communication within the silence of our relationship. When Eddie invited me to "play trains," I did not remain silent. Sitting on the floor with him, I reflected his words, and I made some of my own chugging and whistling sounds. We were doing joint play, and that felt resonant with his shift of attention also.

It is possible to analyze these brief therapeutic moments from a more left-hemisphere perspective. Drawing from the work of Porges and Panksepp, we can see that Eddie's ANS activated into sympathetic mode when he became aggressive toward the baby in his pretend play. During his brief sand tray, Eddie's PLAY system activated, and he discovered that he could deal with his raw feelings of aggression through playing without being judged. As we co-regulated this aggression in the safety of play, this new experience began to offer his neocortex new pathways for managing these raw feelings.

These left-hemisphere principles, once deeply learned, can become a stabilizing foundation operating out of conscious awareness to make room for the flow of resonant responsiveness in the moment, more of a relational, emergent, right-hemisphere process. In contrast with right-based responsiveness, left-hemisphere processing is quite slow, so if I had relied on consciously deciding what to do next,

Eddie and I would have lost that beautiful moment of resonance. Instead, we moved with the embodied, right-hemisphere awareness that aggressive feelings can be managed when they are accepted nonjudgmentally and empathically within a healing relationship.

These intuitive right-brain processes lie at the heart of the psychotherapy process. They operate in the background, beneath the words, and out of conscious awareness. They tap into the implicit affective communications that go back and forth between patient and therapist (Schore, 2011). I would imagine that Eddie's crocodile play emerged more from his implicit knowing than from any conscious explicit knowing. I seriously doubt that he was having conscious thoughts about his baby sister during that interaction. Also, my silent (though fully present) response to Eddie's crocodile play came more from the therapeutic body-to-body connection that taps into the implicit rather than the explicit. Even so, when I take the time to think about it, I can come up with good left-hemisphere explanations for why I responded the way I did.

Perhaps the unique differences of the two hemispheres of the brain can help to explain what happens when we respond "intuitively." Iain McGilchrist (2009) makes a strong case, based on a comprehensive review of brain laterality research, for how each hemisphere creates its own version of the world, each with its own values and priorities, and not necessarily compatible with each other. He explains:

> I believe that the representation of the two hemispheres is not equal, and that while both contribute to our knowledge of the world, which therefore needs to be synthesized, one hemisphere, the right hemisphere, has precedence, in that it understands the knowledge that the other comes to have, and is alone able to synthesize what both know into a useable whole. (p. 176)

The right hemisphere focuses on the space between, on relationships, and is where all new experience enters our brains. Our attachment circuitry is rooted there. All in-the-moment interactions, like this one with Eddie, unfold when we are taking the perspective of the right. The left-hemisphere perspective draws on what the right has experienced and allows us to make systems to organize our world so that we have a sense of what comes next. When the two hemispheres work together, with the right taking the lead with the vision of empathic relatedness and the left creating systems to hold that vision, individuals, families, and societies do well. When we make those split-second intuitive decisions during therapy sessions, or when we say something that almost surprises us as the words come out of our mouths, the right is in the lead, responding to the dance of the relationship. Being deeply attuned in a therapeutic relationship requires our right-hemisphere's mode of affiliation. It may be very akin to what happens to us when we hold a newborn in our arms. We automatically begin speaking in motherese and making faces unlike any that we usually make in our social interactions. Our right hemisphere comes to the fore in the service of composing ourselves in the only way that would make sense to a newborn who is processing primarily from the right hemisphere.

This brings us to the new paradigm of psychotherapy that Allan Schore (2011) has articulated so well for us. From an extensive review of scientific studies and literature, he traces the historical movement of psychotherapy from behavioristic and cognitive modes to interpersonal neurobiological modes in which unconscious affect comes to the fore. He explains:

> Indeed I have suggested that the emotional right hemisphere and not the linguistic left is dominant in the human experience, and that the most fundamental problems of human existence cannot be understood without addressing this primal realm. Over the last two decades a central theme of the body of my studies in developmental psychoanalysis and developmental affective neuroscience has been that the right hemisphere is not only dominant in infancy but over all stages of the life cycle. (p. 8)

The dominance of the right hemisphere for the developing mind does not mean that the left hemisphere is not important in the psychotherapeutic relationship. For example, my left-hemisphere tasks of thorough history taking with Eddie's parents before I saw Eddie in the playroom and my growing knowledge of interpersonal neurobiology were all supportive of my right-hemisphere's intuitive decision. As McGilchrist (2009) points out, the right hemisphere, known for its synthesizing abilities, can speedily make sense of all the left-hemisphere data within relational contexts where micro-seconds count. In therapy, we need both hemispheres dancing in integration with each other. The new paradigm recognizes how we can access more of our resources in relational contexts through the synthesizing right hemisphere.

THE MANY FACES OF PLAY

Like Eddie, most children process their life experiences through pretend play. They use play constantly whenever they have the freedom to do so (and in the process, unknowingly rewire their brains), whether they are dealing with trauma, divorce, adjustments to family changes, or the myriad of other life experiences that impact their developing brains. They use a lot of different types of play, which have been categorized by developmental and social psychologists into the following:

- Early sensory–motor play
- Functional or exploratory play
- Mastery play
- Symbolic play
- Games-with-rules play
- Rough-and-tumble play
- Dramatic play
- Sociodramatic play
- Constructive play

Although numerous psychologists have tried to create developmental taxonomies for these forms of play, Panksepp (1998) suggests that in the interest of having a parsimonious scientific explanation, we might at least contemplate the idea that all of these play variations simply arise from the single motivational system of PLAY called rough-and-tumble play (R & T play) or play fighting. From this primal urge to play, more sophisticated forms of human play emerge in both children and adults through secondary and tertiary processes in the brain. For example, play comes out in adults through verbal interactions that parallel in many ways the R & T play that has been studied in great detail with laboratory animals. Adult play often focuses on verbal interchanges, looking and sounding like friendly teasing as one adult tries to arouse another by provocation, sometimes using sharp and biting comments. There may be several volleys of these kind of exchanges as the two adults try to outdo each other—to see who is cleverer or who can get in the best "punch" line. Panksepp and Biven (2012) use the phrase "sock it to them" to describe what happens in adult verbal play exchanges (p. 366).

These exchanges look and sound a lot like the R & T play of human children or laboratory animals as they run, chase, poke, and flee each other with high-energy behaviors, pretending to kick, wrestle, or hit (open hand) with positive energy and exaggerated movements. Easily reversing roles, chasers become the chased, and winners become temporary losers by handicapping themselves just to keep the play going. Importantly, children signal one another with a "play face," first observed by Harry Harlow (1962) in the social play of rhesus monkeys. The "play face," or as Porges (2011) calls it, the "face-to-face engagement" (p. 276) within the social engagement system, is critical during play in signaling the nonaggressive intent of play fighting (allowing the PLAY system to co-opt the SNS). In contrast, aggression involves shoving, pushing, closed-hand hits, and kicks accompanied by frowns, crying, and menacing facial expressions—signals of moving into the SNS without social engagement.

It is easy to see how sophisticated games such as chess or simpler ones like Candyland involve symbolic fighting. Pulling the "Plumpy" card (meaning, you get sent back to the beginning) in Candyland is definitely a symbolic defeat for one player and a victory for the other. More than once I have had a child in therapy gloat over my demise in such games! Also, dramatic and constructive forms of play incorporate symbolic play fighting involving both successful and failed attempts to resolve conflicts. The hallmark of all these interactions is that they occur within relationship and allow us to test the boundaries of fully engaged, highly energized contact, expanding our windows of tolerance for strong emotions. When we spill over into the danger zone, we are also testing the edges and learning how to pull back into connection again—sometimes with support from others.

PLAY FIGHTING AND EPIGENESIS

Children love boisterous R & T play, and despite the fact that many adults find it disruptive, roughhousing play may be necessary for long-term emotional health. Panksepp (1998) and Sunderland (2006) point out the natural antistress effects and the powerful positive emotional states of this kind of play that are generated due to the strong release of opioids in the brain. This physical interactive play also increases the activation of neural growth factors, such as brain-derived neurotrophic factor (BDNF) and insulin-like growth factor 1 (IGF-1). Panksepp and Biven (2012) say these are like "fertilizers" for the brain. They explain: "It is ever more likely that one of the effects of PLAY activity may be the creation of new prosocial neural pathways in the neocortex through epigenesis—the long-term modification of gene-expression patterns as a function of experience" (p. 380).

Epigenetics helps us to understand the long-standing nature–nurture debate because we now know that gene expression can be turned on or off by environmental experiences. When a dormant gene is turned on in response to experience, it can produce proteins and neuropeptides not previously produced in particular brain cells. The arousal of these neural chemical pathways then modifies brain and mind functions (Panksepp & Biven, 2012, p. 342). This epigenetic process is no clearer than in infant attachment styles (secure and insecure) that develop in response to how the CARE motivational system activates in mothering people. Panksepp and Biven are suggesting that some similar effect on the development of prosocial neural pathways may result from R & T play.

This kind of play has the potential to create a resilient ANS as it expands the window of tolerance for arousal, making room for sympathetic hyperarousal and dorsal vagal hypoarousal without fear. This means that children can experience intense activity and deep rest while remaining in the ventral vagal social engagement system, connected to one another. From another perspective, in R & T play children learn how far they can press another human being and when to back off. Watching the striated facial muscles of their play-fighting partners, they can practice the skills of when to press the accelerator and when to use the brakes of the nervous system. Children are usually better than adults at distinguishing play fighting from aggression (Pellis & Pellis, 2009, p. 147). Although it is easy for play fighting to escalate into real aggression, it is a serious mistake to "throw out the baby with the bath water," to use an old expression. If we continue to ban R & T play at school and at home, we may be discarding a very important embodied activity that mediates an epigenetic influence on prosocial behaviors.

Revisiting the optimal range of play behaviors between infants and mothering people as described by Daniel Stern (1977/2002), we can see that R & T play is even a part of developing the infant's nervous system and self-regulation. Many of the mother–infant games are pretty scary and aggressive symbolically. When a mother or father pretends to be a monster that is going to eat a baby (e.g., "I'm gonna getcha"), it is about as *rough* and *tumble* as you can get. What about the "Rock a Bye Baby on the Treetop" lullaby? How rough can it get if the bow breaks and the baby tumbles when the cradle falls?! And all the fairytales! Most are pretty scary. Fortunately, for the most part, these stories are told within the safe bounds of loving parents teaching their young ones how to build their windows of tolerance for living in a world that can sometimes be highly stressful and even scary.

We do tell stories to children that no doubt help them to stretch the bounds of their nervous systems and their ability to deal with frightening situations. And they tell us stories about their actual adventures in the world as they come to terms with the R & T experiences of life. Often after kids engage in a bout of play, whether it ends in disruption or in great joy, they are eager to share the story with their parents and others. Our left hemispheres need to create and listen to stories, and when we get to build one out of our felt experience, it helps us hold and embody that experience as well as give it shape—and this fairly complex process works best when there is a teller and a listener. On the other hand, when the left hemisphere has to make up a story because it is disconnected from the right (often for want of a listener), then it isn't a coherent story and can block us from staying engaged with our embodied story.

In the next chapter, we are going to turn to storytelling play to explore one of the ways we can make space for keeping the right embodied story connected to the left worded story—and back again. We will meet a group of boys who were adept at telling R & T play stories in their group sand tray process.

Chapter 9

STORYTELLING PLAY

Eleven-year-old Jack caught up with me as I was leaving his school one day after a group sand tray session. He asked, "What's a counselor for?" I replied, "Well, sometimes when kids have a chance to talk to a counselor, it helps them with their feelings." Barely waiting for me to finish, he said, "Yeah, since I have been in this group, I haven't been in no more trouble." The school counselor and I had just finished co-facilitating the fifth session of our sand tray "Friendship Group," in which Jack and five other boys had created and told stories about their sand tray worlds. All of them had been selected for the group because of behavioral or academic problems. Jack was in the group for both reasons. His teacher said that he was behind in all of his schoolwork, he was throwing stones at other kids on the playground, and in general his behavior had seriously deteriorated over the past several months.

During the previous school year, I had been a consultant at this elementary school for a special project to develop a group counseling intervention for children who were identified to be at risk for academic failure because of social–emotional and behavioral problems (Kestly, 2010). The school counselor and I decided to use the sand tray play modality for a pilot group of fifth-grade boys. We introduced the project as a Friendship Group, and at our first meeting we told the boys this: "We know that kids make friends when they play together, so for the next 12 weeks, we are going to come here to play in the sand and tell stories." Clearly they were all surprised, and Tommy voiced it, "You mean, you're just going to let us play?"

Yes, that was exactly what we meant. We were inviting them to "just play" because we wanted to provide an environment in which they could feel safe to internally explore and then possibly verbally express the stories of their lives. We were conceptually focused on helping these young ones find connection and a sense of belonging as their embodied stories were seen, heard, and held by us and each other. We worked from a foundation of believing that off-track behavior and inattention had some roots in internal upset that hadn't yet been allowed to surface in the midst of safe relationship. Drawing primarily from attachment theory and the ideas of Margaret Lowenfeld (1979/1993) (whose child patients created the sand tray process) about thinking in images, we had an intuitive sense that she was right about the nonverbal nature of thought. Lowenfeld was convinced that children could express their inner worlds through images for purposes of healing and mental integration. Once these stories came forward, we believed that the internal relief these children would experience, coupled with a deepened sense of relationship, might lead to helpful changes in behavior and support their academic improvement.

We did not say anything to the boys about why they had been chosen to be in the group. We purposely did not articulate any goals for improved behavior. Nor did we give them a long list of rules for their playtime. Initially, we did ask them to respect each other's play boundaries. Since they would be working in individual trays, we asked them not to touch another child's sand tray world and not to let others touch their own. In the beginning, we simply wanted to create the safety of mutual respect that would allow creative play to flourish. We would have an hour each week when the boys could play freely with the miniatures and sand to create their "worlds," as Lowenfeld (1979/1993) called them. We would use the last twenty minutes to invite the boys to tell stories about their worlds if they chose to do so.

During the pilot project, we listened to the anecdotal reports of changes from the principal, the teachers, the parents, and even from the children themselves. We were eager to refine our intervention protocol. At the end of our pilot group, the school principal asked us if we were interested in expanding the project for the next school year. We were definitely interested. What was behind this request for more? The boys in this first group had been chosen because of fighting on the playground and disruptive behavior in the classroom. The school principal personally knew all of the boys in this pilot group because at some point, each of them had been referred to her for behavior issues. Some of them were "daily visitors" to her office. The group began in January and ended in March. By the middle of April, the principal said that since the group had ended, she had not seen one of the boys from our Friendship Group in her office.

Several teachers also had reported academic improvement in the boys who had been in our group. We were grateful for these reports because we knew that we would need to see both behavioral and academic improvement to justify our novel idea of letting children play during school time. With the support of the principal, we were able to obtain a small grant to expand the project during the following school year. The principal was so convinced of the effectiveness of the group play that she frequently would say to us, "This child needs to be in your sand tray group." That's how we met 11-year-old Jack, struggling with both academics and relationships on the playground.

Close to the end of our 12-week project with Jack's group, I had another unexpected encounter with him. He fell in step with me one day when I was walking down the school hallway. Jack said, "I caught up with all my work." I was very surprised by his comment, since we had never talked in our sand tray group about schoolwork, academic success, or the need for improved behavior at school. Somehow, he associated the playgroup with his ability to stay out of trouble and then to catch up on all of his schoolwork. I checked with his teacher, and she verified that indeed he had caught up on everything. At the beginning of Jack's group, his teacher had been reluctant for him to be pulled out of academic class time because he was so far behind, but she acknowledged that something positive was happening for Jack. Could it have been his participation in the playgroup? She was mystified.

JACK'S SUCCESS—HOW DID IT HAPPEN?

In retrospect, with the abundance of research in interpersonal neurobiology generated during the decade of the brain and since, it has become easier to explain Jack's academic and behavioral improvement. When we initiated our project, we were confident from attachment studies that individual children would benefit emotionally from a sense of belonging, and we were hopeful that the image-thinking process of the sand tray storytelling, elaborated by Lowenfeld, would be beneficial academically.

The work of current neuroscientist Antonio Damasio (1999, 2010) lends support to Lowenfeld's idea of nonverbal thinking. He says that storytelling is a nonlinguistic process that is embedded in the brain's innate tendency to sort, select, assemble, and integrate the objects that we encounter when we engage with our environments. He talks about the naturalness of wordless storytelling (Damasio, 1999):

> Telling stories, in the sense of registering what happens in the form of brain maps, is probably a brain obsession and probably begins relatively early both in terms of evolution and in terms of the complexity of the neural structures required to create narratives. Telling stories precedes language, since it is, in fact, a condition for language, and it is based not just in the cerebral cortex but elsewhere in the brain and in the right hemisphere as well as the left.
>
> Philosophers often puzzle about the problem of so-called "intentionality," the intriguing fact that mental contents are "about" things outside the mind. I believe that the mind's pervasive "aboutness" is rooted in the brain's storytelling attitude. The brain inherently represents the structures and states of the organism, and in the course of regulating the organism as it is mandated to do, the brain naturally weaves wordless stories about what happens to an organism immersed in an environment. (p. 189)

Other neuroscientists have also corroborated Lowenfeld's (1979/1993) idea of the nonverbal nature of thought. Iain McGilchrist (2009) has written extensively about this topic in his book, *The Master and His Emissary: The Divided Brain and the Making of the Western World*. Drawing from a number of scientific studies, McGilchrist explains the unique differences between the right and left hemispheres of the brain along with their similarities and how they collaborate and sometimes inhibit one another.

His example of a bird searching for and obtaining food while looking out for predators provides us with a clear image of why we need two brains (left and right hemispheres) which can and often do function independently, while also coordinating the complex task of looking simultaneously at both the details (left hemisphere) and the overall context (right hemisphere) of the environment. The bird, he says, needs its left hemisphere to focus on picking out one single grain of corn from a field of gravel, and it needs its right hemisphere to simultaneously survey the whole environment for predators. Otherwise, it would be in danger of becoming someone else's lunch.

In a much more sophisticated way, the two hemispheres of the human brain attend to the immediacy of the relational context (right) and later, make orderly sense of that experience (left). We can get a sense of how these two entities offer very different perspectives on events, but also rely on each other to become something that neither one could achieve alone. Good storytelling requires the full participation of both hemispheres, and it requires a special kind of journey through them. Storytelling (as Damasio describes it) begins nonverbally when we humans try to assemble a coherent picture of a "lived" moment as we encounter experiences in our environment or within our memory system. During this "lived" encounter, we experience a "feeling of what happens," and our brains map these bodily feelings in the right hemisphere (Damasio, 1999), creating embodied implicit memories. To bring this experience to the level of language (as McGilchrist, 2009, describes it), it journeys into the left hemisphere where it is "unpacked" and processed in referential form with words that refer to the experience—a re-*presentation* of the experience using language, sophisticated syntax, and bits and pieces of highly focused data. It is then returned to the right hemisphere through metaphorical thinking where once again it finds its connectedness to the world of bodily experience, integrating it with the "feeling of what happens" (in Damasio's terms) through the right hemisphere's unique ability to get the gist of a situation—tone, humor, irony, metaphor, facial expression, and so on. When this full process has occurred, we listeners will get a sense of the meaning of the story in our bodies while hearing the story told in words.

McGilchrist (2009) explains the evolving process of language, as it develops primarily, though not totally, in the left hemisphere. He says that language has increasingly abstracted itself from its origins in the body and in the experiential world. It developed its current form to enable us to refer to whatever is *not present* in experience: language helped its re-*presentation*. . . . In the process important aspects of language, the denotative elements that enable precision of reference and planning, have taken up residence in the left hemisphere, while other aspects of language, broadly its connotative and emotive functions, have remained in the right hemisphere. And the understanding of language at the highest level, once the bits have been put together, the making sense of an utterance in its context, taking into account whatever else is going on, including the tone, irony, sense of humor, use of metaphor, and so on, belongs once again with the right hemisphere. (p. 125)

McGilchrist (2009) is speaking of how words and embodiment can come together to create a narrative with a strong felt sense that can be experienced by both the speaker and the listener. This accords well with his main point that the two hemispheres take different perspectives on the same experience, but that ultimately they can inform each other. He goes on to say this:

Metaphor is the crucial aspect of language whereby it retains its connectedness to the world, and by which the "parts" of the world which language appears to identify retain their connectedness one to another. Literal language, by contrast, is the means whereby the mind loosens its contact with reality and becomes a self-consistent system of tokens. But, more than this, there is an important shape here which we will keep encountering: something that arises out of the world of the right hemisphere, is processed at the middle level by the left hemisphere and returns finally to the right hemisphere at the highest level. (pp. 125–126)

It seems to me, if we follow McGilchrist's (2009) story of the potential relationship between the hemispheres, it would be useful to find a way to collaborate with the way our children's brains and minds work by supporting the nonverbal origins of their thought processes, grounded as they are in bodily experiences. From there we can invite them into the world of the left hemisphere by reflecting their bodily experiences as they present them in gesture, sound, or word. Through our connectedness to them and our more mature system of language, we can mentor them through the processing of the left hemisphere's re-*presentation* of their bodily experiences in language. Following McGilchrist's thinking, we can see that this left-hemisphere language processing then needs to be returned to the right hemisphere through metaphor where the storytelling becomes reconnected to the bodily foundation of meaning-making. If there is sufficient support for the embodied story to become language, the ongoing connection with another fosters development of a natural pathway back to the right hemisphere. This flowing interconnection between the hemispheres allows us to make sense at two levels: in the body and in the knowing. This coherence is often accompanied by a deep sense of settling, which then supports better interpersonal connections and greater capacity for attention.

This right–left–right progression is one of the themes of McGilchrist's (2009) writing and fits well with our storytelling project. Figure 9.1 shows the progression of movement from our right hemispheres (where experience is grounded in nonverbal storytelling) to the left (where we find language to help us express our experiences) and then back to the right for autobiographical and metaphorical understanding: our embodied and coherent story.

Too often in school settings, where learning to read and write is so highly valued, the storytelling gets stuck in the left hemisphere without a chance for returning to the right where integration and meaning take place. Or worse, children are taught language as if it were isolated in the left hemisphere without grounding it in the right hemisphere's bodily experience in the first place. Why is this so? Perhaps it is because our educational system overvalues the analytical and predictive power of language skills, creating a mindset that devalues both embodied experience and the meaning-making process of the right hemisphere. Children are rewarded with praise and good grades if they produce what the left hemisphere is capable of producing on its own—certainty (rules of grammar), facts, correct answers (repetition of what is already known), categories, abstraction, focus, and attention. They are less often rewarded for their right hemisphere's processing of novel stimuli (in response to new experiences), intuitive thinking, dealing with ambiguity, grasping the whole context, and processing information that must be per-

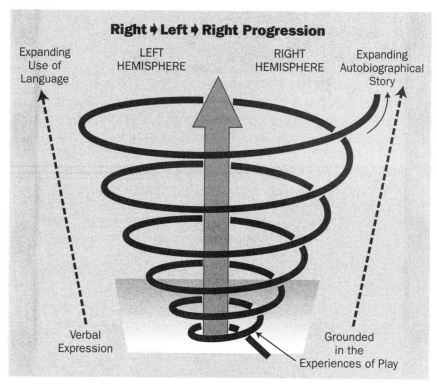

FIGURE 9.1. The Neurobiology of the Storytelling Brain at Play. The right–left–right progression is shown beginning at the bottom right of the diagram where the self (a person's uniqueness or essential being; a person's particular nature) is grounded in the experience of being alive in an environment. This experiencing of self in the right hemisphere moves toward the left hemisphere where it finds verbal expression, and then returns through metaphor to the right hemisphere, where a transformation of the linguistic bits and pieces of information become integrated into an expanding self that feels alive within a dynamic and flowing environment. It is grounded once again in the right hemisphere with its ever-increasing need to move left and then return right. Each time this right–left–right progression takes place, the person is able to tell more and more of his or her autobiographical story, becoming ever more conscious of who he or she is in the world.

ceived in relative terms (e.g., interpersonal relationships, music, art). It is more difficult to measure right-hemisphere specialties, and since schools are more and more being held accountable for measurable student success, it is easy to see why they move in the direction of rewarding left-hemisphere achievements.

I would venture to say that many children who do well in our average public or private schools do so because they are already grounded in patterns of progression from right to left and back to right before they enter school. This pattern is likely established early through secure attachment wherein children become familiar with having their embodied story witnessed by their parents, with the encouragement to share it in words. When these words are reflected without judgment, children naturally develop the capacity to return the full narrative back to the right where it becomes a well-digested part of their history.

Others who do well academically may be fleeing the chaos of their right-hemisphere upset, often resulting from insecure attachment, family challenges, or other kinds of trauma. Sometimes they can find a refuge in school's dominantly left-hemisphere view of knowledge while they continue to struggle relationally. When they are fortunate enough to have a teacher whom they experience as safe and as supporting a sense of connection, they may even begin to repair some of the attachment struggles or traumas. Gradually, they may even build a better capacity to safely listen to their own embodied story and have it heard and witnessed by their teacher, who then "returns" it to their right hemispheres to make their autobiographical narratives fuller and more coherent.

The children who don't do well, such as the boys who were referred to our sand tray group, do not have the right–left–right pattern established prior to attending school and haven't been able to latch onto the left-hemisphere patterns of education. Biologically, however, they begin with an embodied story in their right hemispheres, as we all do, because that is where our constantly unfolding new experiences of life are mediated. If children have little experience with having their lived story witnessed or their worded story held, they won't have developed the neural pathways that make the movement between the hemispheres an easy and natural occurrence. When school forces children into left-mode processing when they haven't yet developed connections to the felt right-mode experience, they have no opportunity to complete the right–left–right cycle. As a result, they may begin to act out or zone out, dropping behind what is expected academically.

All of the boys in our group were struggling in terms of school success, but not one of them had difficulty creating his worldview with the sand tray play and then bringing it to the level of language through storytelling. In the first session or two, most of them were reluctant to talk about their worlds, but when they discovered that we were not critiquing their stories or redirecting them away from the biological necessity of being grounded in their own life experiences, the flow of language could not be stopped. This sequence in our little group points to the naturalness of the progression from right to left and back to right once the right-centered story is welcomed and acknowledged. In some of our groups, we actually had to use egg timers to make sure everyone got a turn to tell the stories of their worlds. Could this simple process of play in a relational context and shared storytelling make such a difference? We think so, provided that the process takes into account the interpersonal neurobiological need of being witnessed in a way that collaborates with the right–left–right progression of the brain–mind.

Once again, we are seeing the motivational systems of PLAY (creating a sand tray world), SEEKING (natural curiosity about novel stimuli), and CARE (adults witnessing and reflecting each child's worldview, and children learning to do the same) coming together in the service of social and emotional growth. Let's look at Jack's progress as he tells stories about his sand worlds in the playgroup.

JACK'S JOURNEY WITH THE JEWELS

It would be possible to tell a story about each fifth-grade boy in Jack's group, but our purposes here are served by following just the stories that Jack told during our 12-week project with his group. He was a special education student, struggling academically and behaviorally. At first he was somewhat shy and rather withdrawn in the group, but during our first session, he told me that he wanted to make an ocean. Having never played in a sand tray before, Jack did not realize that pouring water into the sand tray would result in sand that could not be managed very well, and so he was unable to maintain the shoreline that he wanted for his ocean. Nonetheless, he worked hard on his tray, adding flowers, shells, various kinds of fish, and several handfuls of glass stones (the kind that are often used in aquariums). The more he tried to fix his ocean, the messier it became. He kept adding water, and in the end, it looked like primordial soup, where all the ingredients are stirred together; it was an undifferentiated mess. We invited the boys to tell stories about their worlds, if they chose, during the last 20 minutes of our hour-long session. If they didn't want to say anything about their worlds, they could pass. When it was Jack's turn, he passed.

When the boys came to their second session, we decided that we would have to limit the amount of water they could use in their trays; after the first session, as we cleaned up their trays, we realized that our groups would become unmanageable if we allowed them to have as much water as they wished. When we explained to the boys that they could each have one water bottle to spray their worlds, and that the cap had to stay on, Jack looked stricken. He couldn't decide what to build, and he exhibited anxious behavior, pacing back and forth in front of the sand tray collection, placing things into the tray and then taking them out again. He finally settled on using some rather large zoo animals, and despite his apparent anxiety, he finished about 5 minutes before the other boys. When it was his turn to tell a story, he spoke only two words, "Lion King."

Jack's third and fourth trays were somewhat chaotic and developmentally immature (e.g., lining up many vehicles in a row with no other thematic material). In both sessions, he said little about his worlds. In the fifth session, even though his tray was still pretty chaotic, he told the group the following story: "This is a rich place. People are tearing it down."

We could see that Jack was having a hard time. Because we thought it might be due to our restriction on the amount of water he could use, I offered to have an individual session with him so that we could explore the water issue. I had several trays available: one with sand, one without sand, and a small bucket for carrying water. I told Jack that he could use as much water as he wanted. He began with just enough sand to cover the bottom of the tray, and then he poured water slowly into his tray. He chose a lighthouse and anchored a boat to its shores. He also used many of the same objects that he had chosen for the ocean during our first group session. Only this time, he was able to create a shoreline that differentiated land and sea. There was a remarkable difference between his first ocean and this one, and I could tell that he was really happy.

Our sixth session with Jack's group occurred right after Christmas break, and in keeping with the season, Jack constructed a manger scene from scraps of floor tiles that were in the collection. He used a lot of little trees, shrubbery, all of the nativity figures he could find, and many of the glass jewels that he had used in his two previous ocean scenes. This time he told a short story. He said, "This is Mary and Joseph. Mine is a rich place, except nobody knows about it."

Jack seemed quite invested in making sand trays, and I was curious about his ability to verbalize his trays, so I invited him to do another individual session with me. I laid out all of the photos of his six sand trays and asked him if he would be willing to tell me a story about one of them. He selected the manger scene, and he dictated the following story to me. When he finished, he drew a picture to illustrate the story, and he gave it a title[1] (without any prompting from me), "The Mountains."

> "Once upon a time there was a rich place in the mountains. God was born there. There was a big black door so nobody could come in. But there was a way to get in. It was the corner of the roof.
> "There was a small river for them to drink from so they won't die. There were animals so they could eat so they won't die.
> "There were rich little rocks. They took them to a town, and they sold them to the people for $5.00 each. They were worth $1,000.00 each, but they didn't know. But it was okay that they didn't know. And that's how they lived on."

The very next week (session seven), Jack created a scene with lots of vehicles, gold, and treasures. At the end of the session, he began to play chaotically with the objects in the tray, but he told the following story: "People are stealing gold and stuff. The police are stealing treasures too. People are fighting over the gold."

By this time, Jack was playing with three different themes in his sand trays: God, wealth (gold, treasures, and riches), and the need for water. The God energy appeared for the first time when he made his manger scene, but the water and the "rich little rocks" (aquarium stones) had been there from the very beginning. One of the things

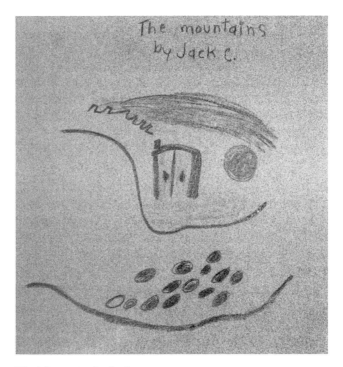

The Mountains by Jack

that is so fascinating to me about the group sand tray process is the way the children or adults begin reflecting one another's thematic material, each in their own way. This happened in Jack's group, notably during the eighth session, during which Jack continued to develop his God and wealth themes. The other boys were also creating trays about God and gold. Stuart filled his tray with treasures to make the point that he was the richest one of all. During this session, Jack created an interesting tray requiring a little ingenuity on his part to convey the idea of God's power, negative though it was. He elaborated this story in greater detail than his previous stories. He said:

> *"This is God. There's the key. They think it is to get out, but the key isn't really. That guy got electrocuted. His body got roasted, except his head. God is sending a message to electrocute him."*

God Sending a Message for Electrocution by Jack

His next tray, during our ninth session, was a peaceful scene with a butterfly resting on top of a chest overflowing with jewels. There were deer (a buck, doe, and two fawns) grazing near a small (plastic) pond filled with water and more treasures. Jack seemed satisfied with his tray, and he elected not to tell a story.

Jack was absent for our tenth session, and as we always did with children who were absent, we placed his name card in his tray to hold his space in our group even though he could not attend. Metaphorically, we wanted to communicate to each boy that his place in our group was unique even when he was not physically present. We would hold him in our minds.

At the next session, Jack sprayed his sand with his water bottle, and he played vigorously with two treasure chests and a horse-drawn wagon train. One treasure chest was half buried in the sand, and the other was sitting on top of it with treasures spilling over the top. His story had only one sentence: "They're taking the gold to town." As he spoke the sentence, he reached into the tray to take the covers off the wagons revealing the rich stones. He had given us a preview of this tray in the story he dictated to me about the manger scene when he told about taking the "rich little rocks" to town where they would be sold for less than their real value.

When we met for our final session, Jack played with his water theme more directly. At the beginning of the session, he brought a 5-inch blue plastic funnel over to me and asked for some tape so that he could make a "pond for the animals." I was doubtful (to myself) that he could seal the end of the funnel to actually hold water, but I found some tape for him anyhow because I wanted to support his creative endeavor. On the right side of his tray he used a lot of veg-etation to create a lush jungle-type environment in which he nestled his pond (his blue funnel with the masking tape). The pond actually held the water! On the left side, he made a desert scene with only one surviving palm tree. He then placed several dinosaurs into his world that were clearly moving from the desert side toward the jun-gle side. Jack revealed in his story how he overcame the water prob-lem—the problem of an environment that could not provide enough water for the animals (dinosaurs). He said: "The dinos are moving to the other side where there is water. T-rex won't let them have any water. The long necks can reach into the water." So despite our restriction of unlimited water, Jack found a way, not only to provide water to the animals that needed it, but also to contain it (in his taped-up funnel pond) to make it a stable, ongoing supply.

To me, this is a profound story of a young boy's struggle to find his self-worth through metaphorically overcoming the obstacles of a life with inadequate resources and too many fears of a punishing God. It is true that his stories lacked verbal detail and that sometimes they were not grammatically correct, but the wordless images were rich in detail and consistent with what his psyche needed. He found a way to contain and then move the jewels that first appeared in his unbounded primordial ocean by putting them into a wagon train to be transported to town. He also came to an understanding of how much the jewels were worth. Even though the jewels were still undervalued by others, he could accept that the people of the town simply did not know. Clearly, he knew, and clearly his journey with the jewels, with us as witness to his journey, helped him to find and internalize the treasures within, coming into an acceptance of his own worth.

If we consider his sand tray images as we might ponder the meaning of a dream, we can see that Jack was willing to move into an environment (the lush jungle) where water was available to him (and the thirsty animals). He was able to adapt for the sake of finding what he needed. His encounter with God was electrifying! Through playing (activating his SNS), he was able to modulate his overwhelming fears of a punishing God through the social engagement of play where he could check the faces of his peers and the school counselor and me to make sure that God's electrocution was really "just play."

These are my metaphorical musings, but what we know for sure is that his behavior at school improved remarkably, and that he caught up with all of his academic work. He took his metaphorical journey with the jewels from his undifferentiated ocean to the underground treasure chest, then to the above-ground chest overflowing with treasures, and finally to the town where they could be valued. He also found a way to get the water he needed. He took this journey within the socially engaged Friendship Group where we focused on connection and safety. We never talked to him about his negative behavior or his poor grades. He did, however, feel the need to tell me about his good behavior and his academic improvement once he realized these troubling areas were changing. Somehow, to him, it was a result of being in the playgroup. At least, that is how he reported it to me, "Since I have been in this group, I haven't been in no more trouble." He also said at a later time, "I caught up all my work."

I believe the structure of the playgroup allowed him to proceed with what McGilchrist (2009) calls the right–left–right progression through the divided brain. The play format allowed him to begin each session in his right hemisphere, where his brain could map his life experiences as he grounded them in the bodily activity of playing with the miniatures and sand. Each time he created a sand world, he had a visual image and a bodily "felt sense" of a "wordless story," and from there it seemed so natural for it to make its way into the left hemisphere, where the images and felt experiences were "unpacked" through narrative and other analytical processes. Jack and all the other boys seemed to need language to explain and share what they had created in their play—especially when they realized that we would not critique their use of language.

The counselor and I entered into intersubjective relationships with them through witnessing their stories and reflecting their metaphors and the rhythm and tones (prosody) of their speech—whatever we could do to let them know that we could feel what they were feeling. We tracked them closely as they presented their worlds. We avoided any "lessons" or any indication that they should rethink their re-*presentations* of their left-hemisphere narratives. We really wanted to fully support the creative process (or what McGilchrist [2009] would call the right–left–right progression).

If we resonated with their left hemisphere narratives within the intersubjective realm, we believed that the boys would know (via their "felt" experience) that the narrative of the left hemisphere is a wonderful tool for "grasping" that leads to understanding, both for them and for us during the community storytelling. Through this shared activity, they could then make sense of their life experiences, allowing them to return to their right hemispheres. Here, in this primary hemisphere, McGilchrist (2009) says, we use metaphor to process at the highest level. We make meaning of our lives in the context of the whole.

In the next chapter we are going to explore more of the neurobiology of storytelling so that we can talk about how we as therapists, parents, and teachers might compose ourselves in ways that collaborate with the brain's natural love of, or as Damasio (1999) says, its "obsession" for telling stories. Remembering that verbal narratives have their roots in wordless storytelling, we will reconnect with Alice, whom we met in Chapter 1. We will hear the wordless story of her first 10 months in an orphanage as she uses the play medical kit to listen to her mother's heartbeat.

CHAPTER NOTE

1. I am careful not to elicit verbal material (such as asking for a title) too quickly from children (or adults) because it can sometimes take them away from the necessary right-hemisphere processing.

Chapter 10

THE INTERPERSONAL NEUROBIOLOGY OF STORYTELLING PLAY

When we first met Alice in Chapter 1, she was just 6 years old. She was playing with the wolf and dolphin puppets, and the alligator with the zippered mouth, telling her trauma story of dental surgery and why it was so difficult for her to talk at school. She actually used very few words during that dramatic puppet play, but I could see that she was delighted and relieved for us to be able to co-narrate the story through our actions.

Being mindfully present and knowing Alice's early history, I could receive her narrative at multiple levels in my mind. I could understand with my left hemisphere that she was working on trauma, and in my right hemisphere, I could feel the branches of her nervous system (her sympathetic and ventral vagal parasympathetic) collaborating as her PLAY system came online to deal with her deep bodily fears of talking. I could sense my social circuitry attuning to her, delighting in our "pretend" mode of play. This resonance allowed Alice's brain to activate the circuitry where her implicit traumatic memories were stored. Within the safety of play and our attuned relationship, her right-mode emotional and behavioral responses helped her open the neural nets of terror and abandonment related to her dental surgery. The presence of both her own embodied experience of the trauma (within her window of tolerance) and my embodied experience of providing safety and accompaniment allowed these circuits to open, creating the conditions to help her modify these deeply ingrained neural nets (Ecker et al., 2012). The arrival of my offer of safe presence right at the time when the terror of her trauma was active is called a *disconfirming experience*.

In this chapter, we are going to deepen our exploration of play narratives by following Alice's story of her earlier traumas. In this context, we will talk about the science of changing implicit memories and how that process is supported during storytelling play—stories with and without words.

In her "dental surgery" puppet story, Alice used a few words, but for her earliest trauma story, there were no words at all. She had only implicit memories. Nonetheless, as we commenced this phase of therapy (with her mother in the playroom most of the time), she was able to show us the story of her first 10 months in an overcrowded and understaffed orphanage. She did it without words through her play and in the way she related to her mother and me. I could see how important these stories were because they made visible the implicit mental models that underlay her challenging behaviors.

Although Alice was beginning to talk at school and rarely got in trouble there, her behaviors at home were difficult for both of her parents and her two older siblings. Alice resisted bedtime rituals— the nightly bath, the teeth brushing, and attempts by her mother to soothe her with back rubs, bedtime stories, and cuddling. She hoarded food in her bedroom even though she was allowed to have snacks most anytime in the kitchen. She sometimes kicked the family dog, and she frequently challenged family rules. Alice also could behave like a model child at times. She was charming, and fortunately, adults found her delightful. Peers mostly ignored her (and she ignored them) because she was inept at the give-and-take that relationships require. Her parents were devoted to her, but it was hard for Alice to give much in return. Mrs. Murray described the "emptiness" she felt in her relationship with Alice compared to her two older (biological) children who were thriving and developmentally on track.

From the beginning of Alice's therapy, her mother and I had worked separately on a number of strategies to help her co-regulate Alice's behavior, to strengthen their attachment relationship through deepening Mrs. Murray's understanding of intersubjectivity (letting Alice know that she could feel what Alice was feeling as they shared activities together with the same intention), and coaching her on how to be helpful during the play therapy times when she participated in a session to work on attachment issues. Mrs. Murray was highly educated and very motivated to help Alice, and although I had coached her on how to approach the relationship play with Alice during the therapy sessions, the play sometimes became challenging and sometimes deeply moving. Alice began to exhibit some very infantile needs during the play sequences with her mother, showing us the story of how "unmothered" she had been in her first 10 months. Here is how it began.

Not long after the puppet play sessions, I introduced drumming play to Alice and her mother. I brought my "real" stethoscope and three drums into the playroom. By this time Alice knew that I was not a "real" doctor—or at least, not the kind that gave shots—so I thought it would be okay to play a little with the real stethoscope. I handed it to her mother and asked her to find Alice's heartbeat. When she could hear it, I instructed her to tap out the beat with her other hand so that I could see and then play the rhythm of Alice's heartbeat. I began drumming the beat softly and said, "Alice, this is the rhythm of your heart. It is beating just like this." I was drumming a double thump because that was how her mother tapped it out to me. I asked Alice to drum her heartbeat with me. She could do it, and I gave her mother the other drum so that she could join in. I continued playing my drum, shifting over to a single pulse while they played the double thump of Alice's heartbeat. Alice smiled slightly.

I said, "Okay, let's trade." We traded drums (each was a little different), and Alice's mother gave her the stethoscope. I quickly explained to Alice that the listening device of the real stethoscope was a loud amplifier of sound, and that it was important not to make loud sounds into the chest piece. I told her that the person with the earphones in their ears also had to be the one holding the chest piece ("in your ears / in your hand"). By this time I knew Alice well enough to know that she could follow most instructions. (*Note*: I never allow children to play with the real stethoscope without monitoring it closely because of potential ear injury).

We repeated the listening and echoing for the mother's heartbeat.

Alice seemed to be particularly fascinated with her mother's rhythm, and I wondered if she was listening with the feelings of a very young baby or even a child in the womb. We did this for about 5 minutes. In the following session, we used the stethoscope again, this time checking Alice's heartbeat before and after she ran up and down the sidewalk just outside the playroom for about 20 seconds. We played the slow heartbeats (before running) and the fast ones (after running) on the drum. I talked briefly to Alice and her mother about how our hearts send messages to our brains about what is happening in our bodies. We talked a little about how several long conscious breaths could help to send messages to our brains to slow down and get calm again.

Most of the time in play therapy sessions, I follow the lead of the child, but occasionally, when I believe it might be helpful, I will introduce a specific idea and then wait to see if the child latches on. In this case, I was trying to help Alice develop some strategies for calming herself. To avoid over-leading, I did not bring the drums or stethoscope to the next session. Alice, however, had already latched on. She got the play medical kit out and pretended to listen to her mother's heart. She then discovered the blood pressure device in the play kit and spent some time figuring out how to take her mother's blood pressure. This involved a lot of bodily contact with her mother. In the course of the play, she began touching her mother's cheeks in a way that looked like an infant who had just discovered the joy of reaching out for her mother's face. I could tell that her mother was surprised and deeply touched by these gestures. What a beautiful story of tentative but real connection was beginning to unfold.

Mrs. Murray had told me previously that Alice was usually averse to touching. She did not like hugs and seldom wanted to hold hands. When her mother would reach out to her, she often reacted quickly by pulling her hand or shoulder away. During this session, however, she seemed curious about her mother's face—just a little. Perhaps in the safety of these relationships, her infant needs were reawakening. As she was free to touch her mother when she was ready, maybe she was beginning to activate the attachment circuitry that had been both starved and shaped for avoidance during her time in the orphanage. As her mother welcomed the touch with her heart open, Alice could feel and see that the offer of connection was received— exactly what had been needed and not available when she was an infant. A powerful disconfirming experience was arising naturally within the play.

Mrs. Murray also told me that Alice was unable to drink from a bottle when they adopted her at 10 months of age unless she was facing away from her mother's face, or unless the bottle was propped beside her. These fixed behaviors had their own story to tell, and coupled with the fact that her head was flat on one side when they adopted her, we believed that she had been profoundly neglected during her first 10 months. It was clear to me that she likely missed most of the eye gazing that goes on between infants and mothers during the first 6 months of life. She probably had none of the babbling and interactive play that Daniel Stern (1977/2002) describes as the "dance" between mother and infant that teaches the preverbal baby the moves of social interaction necessary for human communication (e.g., rhythm, turn taking, the variations in tempo, and the initiation, maintenance, termination, or avoidance of interactions).

Right after Alice touched her mother's face, she got the set of play dishes off the shelf and said, "Let's make a picnic." She set two places with play food and drinks. She pretended to eat and drink, making loud slurping sounds, and she instructed her mother to do the same. Mrs. Murray complied. Then Alice took a piece of the fruit and held it up to her mother's mouth, "Here, eat this." Next she asked her mother to feed her. It lasted just a few moments, but I was deeply moved as I witnessed this tender exchange. Alice broke the tension of the pretend feeding with some baby-like babbling sounds that the mother quietly reflected. We were beginning to be able to move in and out of the stories unfolding from various developmental stages quite smoothly—from 6-year-old to infant and back, making it safe for Alice to continue to share her wordless story of infancy while developing a new capacity for mutual play.

During their joint play sessions, I modeled reflective communication and attunement with Alice and explained to her mother why it was so important to create a permissive environment in the playroom, with limit setting only when necessary. When Alice demanded that her mother play a certain way, I would simply reflect, "You want to make sure your mother does it just the way you do." With modeling and coaching, Mrs. Murray developed a sensitive, highly attuned, and flexible style of interacting with Alice. When the infantile behaviors emerged, however, the mother and I had to spend more time around the importance of attunement: the kind of attunement that we naturally accord infants. It was a delicate balance to respond to the infant behaviors (babbling, hide-and-seek games, and infant-style touching) emerging in Alice's almost 7-year-old body. Sometimes Mrs. Murray was at ease with the infant behaviors, but at others, she felt awkward and confused. We talked about how she could contain these behaviors if Alice made a bid for this kind of play at home or in public places by giving Alice a special time and place for them, with limits that made sense to Mrs. Murray. We also explored how she felt in her own body when Alice initiated the infant behaviors.

Over a period of about 4 months, Alice was highly motivated to have these joint play sessions with her mother. She used a variety of play themes and modalities, and directed her mother's actions closely when they were involved in joint play. She especially liked making sand trays with her mother. She would often use vehicles and set up racetracks showing her mother exactly how to play and what kind of sounds to make. I witnessed and reflected their play, modeling attuned communication so that Alice could sense that her mother was feeling with her. In a relaxed ventral vagal state, our mirror neurons and resonance circuits take in the feeling of the other person and reflect it back nonverbally through the look in our eyes, the sound of our voice, and the language of our bodies. As time passed, I encouraged and coached her mother to take over these reflective responses. She understood Alice's need for this specific kind of communication, and she got very good at it. A new experiential narrative about the possibility of sustained connection was clearly emerging in their bodies and actions toward one another.

Reflecting on this whole period of time, I have my own narrative of what was occurring in our play. First, I was deeply touched by the orphanage story that Alice was telling us. She, of course, had no explicit memory of her time there, but she was showing us what she needed and did not get during those first 10 months. I have no doubt about the quality of care that Alice received from her adoptive family, but her young nervous system was not ready for the intimate mother–infant play when she first came into their home, and her behaviors were in the tight grip of her implicit memories. The patterns of rejection and helplessness that developed when she reached out and failed to connect were deeply engrained, and it must have been natural for Alice to defend herself or dissociate when her adoptive family tried to interact with her in intimate human communication. It is easy to mistake infant dissociation for calmness, and so Alice was likely able to continue this strategy without her parents understanding that she was in a collapsed state, so she spent too much time in hypoarousal.

In addition, other developmental issues, such as delayed language, came to the fore, and so the early infant–mother dance of play had to wait. Clearly the longing never went away, and finally Alice got her chance to tell her earliest wordless story. It was a powerful narrative because it formed the core of a mental model that Alice was using to navigate the world. Unfortunately, it was a mental model without the reciprocity patterns of human communication that Stern (1977/2002) describes as the task of the first 6 months of life. It was a right-hemisphere story with no words, and we simply needed to engage with her from our right hemispheres, allowing our left-hemisphere grasp of Alice's history and our evidence-based and science-informed knowledge to support intuitive decisions that would emerge spontaneously as we played with her. We would need to continue to attune consistently to her deep biological longing for social connection.

THE NEUROBIOLOGY OF NARRATIVES

Bonnie Badenoch (2011) describes some important clues about the biological nature of storytelling narratives:

> We are storytelling beings; the propensity for meaning is written into our genes. Our brains drive us to make meaning of our experiences, resolve conflicts, and prepare for the future. It has also become clear that this activity does not begin when we consciously shape experience into language. The internal process of knitting together neural networks related to our history and its impact on what we will do next goes on all the time, below the level of conscious awareness. (p. 83)

She cites research by Raichle (2010) documenting the amount of energy the brain uses for this internal weaving process as we make sense of our past histories, preparing us continuously for what is to come. The present moments of weaving past and future in storytelling mode go on all the time even when we are consciously busy with other tasks. Badenoch (2011) identifies the circuits involved in this integrative process: (1) the medial parietal cortex (an area that helps us remember events relevant to our personal lives), (2) the medial prefrontal cortex (concerned with self-reflection and autobiographical memory), and (3) the posterior cingulate cortex (an integrating region located near the back of the brain).

Researchers (Gusnard & Raichle, 2001; Raichle, 2010) call these circuits our "default network." Looking back at our sand tray Friendship Groups (see Chapter 9), I now know that these default networks were active all the time when the children were playing together. We never asked them to build sand trays in silence because it felt counterintuitive to the group play process. Children would talk about all sorts of things while they played. They would be telling each other about the latest movie they saw, or what someone else had said on the playground, and so on. Meanwhile, they were using their hands to create their worlds in the sand, and the stories they told during our formal storytelling time appeared to have no correlation with the "chatter" of their free playtime. Their narratives went deep, revealing their life histories metaphorically with great accuracy. We could see the internal weaving process of the default networks at play. Now that I reflect, I believe that part of the reason these boys were able to descend so deeply into their life histories was the fact that their left hemispheres were occupied with the chatter of their peer interactions, freeing their right hemispheres to have dominance as they played bodily in the trays.

Clearly, Jung (1989/1961) had some intuitive understanding of the neurobiology of how our storytelling brains work. He recounted his personal story of the importance of his own embodied play in *Memories, Dreams, Reflections*. In response to a period of disorientation in his adulthood, he consciously chose to play as he had when he was eleven years old, using stones, mud, and other natural materials to make a whole village on the shore of the lake near his home. He was attempting to connect with the creativity he had known as a child. He related the following.

I went on with my building game after the noon meal every day, whenever the weather permitted. As soon as I was through eating, I began playing, and continued to do so until the patients arrived; and if I was finished with my work early enough in the evening, I went back to the building. In the course of this activity my thoughts clarified, and I was able to grasp the fantasies whose presence in myself I dimly felt.

Naturally, I thought about the significance of what I was doing, and asked myself, "Now, really, what are you about? You are building a small town, and doing it as if it were a rite!" I had no answer to my question, only the inner certainty that I was on the way to discovering my own myth. For the building game was only a beginning. It released a stream of fantasies which I later carefully wrote down. (pp. 174–175)

Jung described how foolish he felt to return to the games of his childhood, but he also realized how crucial it was. He said,

I had no choice but to return to it and take up once more that child's life with his childish games. This moment was a turning point in my fate, but I gave in only after endless resistances and with a sense of resignation. For it was a painfully humiliating experience to realize that there was nothing to be done except play childish games. (p. 174)

These play experiences were a turning point in Jung's life, and it gives us a window (from an adult point of view) into the wisdom of children's embodied play. They seem to know intuitively what Jung was able to express with language—that play is essential in finding one's way. When children are given the safety and freedom to express themselves, their default networks help them tell the critical stories of their lives. Alice is a good example. She was showing us (telling us without words) her core story. Her default networks were serving her well.

Badenoch (2011) explores another aspect of this process that is very important regarding the brain circuitry of narratives. She explains:

As tenacious as this network is in integrating everything available to it, it is likely that circuits that remain disassociated from the overall flow of the brain stay literally out of the loop of the default network. This is such an important understanding, because it points the way toward the heart of therapeutic work. (p. 83)

As we attuned to Alice, she led us to the heart of our therapeutic work together. By initiating the play themes and directing her mother's play, she "told" us about the implicit orphanage story of abandonment that was driving her behavior. In her hours alone in her orphanage crib, she no doubt passed from disconnection into separation distress, fear, and possibly rage (Panksepp & Biven, 2012), over and over, and finally fell into dissociation when her helpless inability to attract someone to attend to her became too overwhelming. With enough experiences like that, dissociation may have become a well-worn adaptive neural pathway. Now, it looked as if her capacity for dissociation was helping her to seal off painful experiences of profound abandonment.

More than once I observed her collapse onto the floor during a play session, and Mrs. Murray described numerous incidents of daily life where Alice appeared to be using this core adaptation: freezing and becoming nonresponsive when the normal demands of family life overwhelmed her. For example, her father had to physically pick her up one day and put her in the car to avoid being late for a piano lesson. Alice loved music and generally was eager to go to her lessons, but on this particular day she was playing a game on her computer and did not want to stop. When her father insisted and physically picked her up, it may well have triggered early implicit memories of her attempts to reach for connection that so often resulted in failure to get her needs met. Now, years later in a very different situation, her sensory system may have triggered this implicit feeling of having her deep needs and desires cut short. In the car, she sat frozen, staring ahead, and acting as if she did not hear her father's request to put on her seat belt (or perhaps really not hearing his request).

Although her refusal to talk in the car may have made her appear to be a "spoiled and obstinate child," if we look deeper, we can see that she was probably responding as she did in the crib when her needs weren't met: by dropping into a dorsal vagal state of disconnection from herself and others. This behavior pattern is a huge dilemma and very frustrating for parents who are trying to provide structure and a well-regulated life for a child. Unfortunately for all of them, the deep implicit adaptation of withdrawal in the face of massively unmet needs could be triggered now by what someone without her history would experience as a normal, mild stressor. Also, without the early bonding followed by the normal individuation, she did not learn how to engage in the patterns of reciprocity of human communication to get her needs met. Because her emotional development was still at the infant stage, she could have little or no experience of herself as a separate person in relationship to others. In babies, we find this merged oneness endearing, but in an almost 7-year-old, we may experience it as unpleasant. Reflecting her father's understandable inability to receive her in this state, Alice could easily become unpleasant with him as well.

After several of these interactions, we began to look at these patterns in a different way, going back to Stern's (1977/2002) idea that play interactions between mothering people and their infants during the first 6 months of life provide core experiences that affect brain development in three important ways: (1) Gazing is one of our earliest forms of human relatedness (according to Stern, mothers and infants always gaze at each other during play); (2) interactive play lays the foundation for reciprocal patterns of human communication; and (3) optimal play arousal helps to build windows of tolerance in the ANS. If Alice had few or maybe no opportunities for gazing or relational play in her first 10 months in the orphanage, we can see that she was missing the essential experiences that strengthen an optimally functioning social engagement system (the ventral vagal branch of the ANS). Instead, she was likely spending most of her time in sympathetic fear arousal or dorsal vagal helpless collapse, so these pathways became very strong and easily accessible (again, neurons that fire together, wire together). Now, her capacity for social engagement could close off in an instant, leaving her in either fight–flight or collapse. She also had an implicit expectation that when people did approach her, it would not be to connect with her but to simply do whatever minimally needed to happen to maintain life, but without any acknowledgment of her emotional needs.

In psychodynamic terms, Alice had not had the experiences that would allow her first to bond to a significant other (approximately the first year of life) and then develop a healthy sense of a separate self through the process of individuation (approximately the second year of life) (Mahler, Pine, & Bergman, 1975; Schore, 1994). We develop our sense of "I" through first having a rich experience of "we," in which we receive sufficient reflection of ourselves to emerge from oneness with our mothers. Until that "I" could be established through experiences such as touching her mother's face and being lovingly received, Alice couldn't begin to develop a reliable capacity for the relational back-and-forth of daily interactions. When the implicit memory of her earliest relationships began to emerge in the safety of the playroom, she had room to explore what her infant self had always needed, first as a "we" and then as an "I" in relationship to others.

THE SCIENCE OF NEURAL CHANGE

The challenge for our play therapy initially was to help Alice find a way to bring the dissociated networks of trauma and abandonment into the play. Relying on Porges's (2011) polyvagal theory, we knew that this could happen if we provided safety, because then Alice's nervous system would be able to detect these conditions of safety through neuroception (nonconscious knowing). Once she felt safe, we knew that her attachment circuitry would come more fully online, bringing the earlier implicit experiences of abandonment to the fore, along with her legitimate need for being seen and felt in her infant state. Her reach for deep intimate connection would manifest once again, perhaps almost undetectably at first, but if we could catch it and respond to it, she would try again and again in more complex ways.

We could also draw from Badenoch's (2011) beautiful synthesis of scientific studies about how neural change takes place:

> Studies have shown that when an implicit memory in long-term storage is actively responding to current perceptions—meaning that the neural circuit in right-mode processing holding the memory is activated and producing an emotional or behavioral response—*and* if, in addition, current perceptions clearly contradict the mental model contained in this implicit memory, then the *synapses of the memory circuit can move from a locked state into a malleable state in which new energy and informa-*

tion can fundamentally rewrite them, eliminating the original mental model from implicit memory. This process of updating an implicit memory, which neuroscientists term *reconsolidation,* may allow for a variety of opportunities for change, as we shall see. When a newly revised memory is restored, or reconsolidated, it *contains* a different implicit pattern with *modified* bodily sensations, behavioral impulses, emotions, perceptions, and global mental models, including models of relationship to self and others— the now-familiar ingredients of implicit memory. (pp. 186–189, emphasis in original)

As implicit memory changes, so does our felt narrative. Behavior, another form of our story, reflects the implicit changes, and eventually we may even develop a new spoken narrative. We are going to use several examples of Alice's play sequences to illustrate the three aspects of neural change described by Badenoch. These are (1) memory differentiation, (2) contact with emotionally vivid experience, and (3) adding disconfirming energy. You can explore this topic further and see some examples from work with adults in Badenoch's *The Brain-Savvy Therapist's Workbook* (2011).

The first aspect, *differentiating the implicit memory,* can be seen over a number of joint sand tray sessions created by Alice and her mother. Alice began one particular session by saying, "What should we play, Mom?" Mrs. Murray answered, "Mmmmm, you want to know what we should play. What do you think?" Alice knew that Mrs. Murray loved dirt bikes, so she found some motorcycles, and said, "What about these?" Mom agreed, and then Alice began preparing the landscape (wet sand) by making racetracks. She built two of them, and she spent a long time making sure the tracks were exactly alike and that each one had a starting place, a pit stop, and a finish place. She used some of the detailed clay tools to carefully rake the sand, redoing the lines many times to make sure they were just right.

I noticed her labored breathing and her highly focused attention, signaling increased arousal in her nervous system and the possibility that she was beginning to move toward more *vivid emotional contact* with the realm of her implicit memories. I said very little, and when I did speak, I used soft tones because Alice was murmuring softly to herself, and she was very intent. I said, "You want it to be just right." She answered in a tiny, almost inaudible voice, "Yeah." In this reflective exchange, we were building the relational foundation of her feeling seen so she might move more fully into her earlier experience.

Finally, she was ready for the race with her mother. Mrs. Murray followed instructions from Alice precisely. She moved her motorcycle just slightly behind Alice's, making the same vehicle sounds that Alice made and making sure Alice won most of the time. In this interaction, she was likely providing a *disconfirming experience* of attuned play of the kind Alice had not been able to have as a very young one. At the end of the session, I said, "Alice, you made one track for your mother, and one for yourself so that you each had your own track for your race that you did together." I believe Alice was working on differentiating self and other at a metaphorical level by making two tracks that mirrored each other almost perfectly.

These sand experiences were interlaced with other times when Alice was engaging in infant repair experiences with her mother (such as those described above), so we were moving back and forth between meeting her infant needs and supporting her push toward safe differentiation. From her earliest experience, all she knew about someone moving away was that it resulted in disastrously painful and frightening feelings of abandonment and rejection of her very being. Now, she was exploring moving away within the safety of these holding relationships.

Alice pursued this theme for about 4 weeks (including many variations). During this time, Mrs. Murray told me that they were beginning to have some enjoyable days together, and that to her surprise, Alice actually kissed her. She also drew a picture titled, "Our Family." Mrs. Murray said there were still plenty of challenges, but she was beginning to get a glimpse of how it might feel to enjoy being with Alice.

As our play continued, we began to see increased *contact with emotionally vivid experience*. Alice continued with the differentiating play activities, but the emotional relatedness of her play became more energized. This increased relatedness told us that her window of tolerance for emotional intensity was growing larger, and that perhaps the mental models that held her core embodied experience that relationships are dangerous were changing significantly. She shifted the "dirt bike" theme by having the motorcycles begin to talk to each other. With an animated voice, Alice's bike said, "Hey, do you want to be my friend?" "Oh yes!" said Mrs. Murray's bike. Alice invited her new friend to come over to her house (continuing dialogue between Alice and her mother), and when the friend came, she made a place for both of them to sleep. As she carefully and tenderly spread sand over the two bikes, she said (stepping back to take a third-person position), "This is their blanket." At this point, she is both participant and observer of the play. She continued the differentiating part of the play by marking off little areas in the sand (forming walls with the wet sand) as if they were different rooms (multiple bedroom spaces), and she continued the emotionally vivid play with a new level of emotional tone in her voice. I believe Alice may have been contacting the early implicit memories of reaching out for human connection in the orphanage (multiple bed spaces, and desire for being comforted by the relational pairs being soothed into a state of sleep).

Fortunately for Alice, during this play sequence, Mrs. Murray provided her with the third aspect of neural change, *adding disconfirming energy*. She was attuned, and she responded to Alice in a way that Alice could hear the words and feel the feelings of a mother receiving her deep infant longing to connect. I believe that Alice's neural net of abandonment opened, and that her mother was willing to resonate with Alice's play to provide her with an experience that disconfirmed the old experience of rejection associated with reaching and failing to connect. During these "friend dialogues," I noticed that Alice was no longer breathing in a labored manner, indicating that she and her mother had moved into a dance of co-regulation. I was deeply touched, and even though I knew that we would need to repeat these play sequences a few or maybe even many times, I could see that Alice's core neurobiological system was resonating with her mother's, a process that leads to the development of integrative pathways to support attachment and healthy relatedness.

One of the things Alice loved to do during our therapy sessions was play games. She especially liked the game Trouble, and she sometimes wanted to play the board game Sorry. In one particular session, she showed us how adept she was at being all alone (as she probably was in the orphanage) even in the presence of others. We were taking turns in a Sorry game, and it was going along nicely. I was paying attention to using my skills of reflection and attuned communication (letting her know that I could feel what she was feeling while we were jointly focusing on the same thing, with the intention to have fun together). Alice said, "Here, Mom, let me help you." She took a card from the center of the board (for her mother), read it, and then moved her mother's piece. I thought she was just allying with her mother in an attempt to secure family ties as I had observed in prior board game sessions. However, after several rounds of taking both her turn and her mother's turn, she began taking my turn as well. Suddenly, I realized that Mrs. Murray and I were both spectators to her playing Sorry all by herself. Inside I wept, realizing that she had spent a great deal of her life in the presence of others being almost entirely alone.

I wanted to provide Alice with some accurate feedback about our "joint" (or not so joint) play. I said, "So you don't really need your mom and me to play this game." She ignored me. A few minutes went by, and I said, "I'm bored. I don't like playing when I can't move my own pieces." Mrs. Murray, picking up on my cue, pretended to snore. Alice said, "Mom, wake up!" But Alice continued to move our pieces. We were at the end of our session time, and Alice was reluctant to stop playing—even though she was playing all alone. She was clearly telling us a story about something and really wanted us to hear what it was. I had assumed that she was showing us her aloneness, but in retrospect, as I think about it, it may be that Alice was seeing us as extensions of herself (as would an infant in the first year of life), and may not have experienced aloneness at all. Maybe, in the absence of reciprocity skills, she was just unable to get into our shoes to take our perspectives—to know that we would want our own experiences of participating in the game. We will never be able to put Alice's wordless story into words that can hold all the nuances of what she was telling us. It is possible that both of these versions—and more—were present during our play.

Over the next week, I thought a lot about my "boredom" intervention, and I realized that this response was probably not helpful no matter what story she was sharing in her play. When Alice returned the following week, I decided to offer a repair. I said, "Alice, I have been thinking about our Sorry game that we played last week. I was so amazed at how well you played all three of our pieces, but your mom and I wanted to play with you, and then we got bored because we weren't moving our own pieces." Alice was fiddling with the medical kit, appearing somewhat uninterested in what I was saying. After a few moments, I continued, "I've been wondering about how you could have gotten so good at playing all by yourself." She looked up and shrugged her shoulders. I said, "I'm wondering if you got good at playing all by yourself when you were a baby in the orphanage. I think your nannies must have been pretty busy taking care of lots of babies." Alice did not respond. I let a few moments go by and then said, "You know, most babies learn to play when their moms and dads teach them how to do it. So I've been thinking that your mom and I could show you how we can play these games together so that your mom and I can have fun, too. The next time we play a game, your mom and I will be sure to stay awake and play our own pieces so that we don't get bored."

Alice seemed to ignore my attempt to repair, but as time would tell, she gradually became more willing to let her mother and I take our turns, and of course, we were much more attentive about being enthusiastic play partners, giving her plenty of attunement as we played. Despite the fact that that I pretended to be bored during what appeared to be Alice's solitary play, I was playing close attention to her and to the feelings that were arising in me. Although my initial intervention turned out not to be helpful, the close attention to her and to myself within our relationship eventually helped me to find a better way to be with Alice around her solitary play.

Again, looking at this example, we can see the potential for neural change in this play sequence. When I looked back on the board game session, I realized why I had made the "boredom" comment. In that moment, I experienced myself being put on the outside of a relationship, and I reacted by latching onto an old idea of "providing accurate feedback" instead of staying present to the *emotionally vivid experience* that Alice was presenting. I dropped out of relationship and into technique, and for Alice this response was probably confirming rather than *disconfirming of her early experiences* of playing alone. Fortunately, we are not required to get it right 100% of the time, and when we don't get it right the first time, we can try again and offer to repair the relationship. In fact, Stern (1977/2002) says that missteps in the dance can build resilience if we are able to spot the inevitable ruptures to relationship and offer repair.

On that note, I also want to say that Carl Rogers' idea of providing accurate feedback is often very useful. In some situations, even in another board game session with Alice, my feedback of boredom might have been just the right thing. With Alice's history, however, and the way she was playing in that particular session, the boredom response was probably just one more confirmation that she was not worthy of having engaged play partners. It also underscores for me just how challenging it is for parents and therapists to stay present in relationship with an older child who has not learned the patterns of reciprocity.

In my attempt to repair with Alice, I was hoping that we would get more opportunities for neural change during board game playing. And we did! Such opportunities were predictable because Alice really loved these board games, and the structure they provided also allowed her to step back from the emotional encounters she was having in the sand trays with her mother. I think she needed this structure following the sand tray wherein the vehicles were tying to become friends. The next time we played a board game, Mrs. Murray and I were both vigorous about preserving our turn taking. We did it in playful ways in order to support our intent to have fun and also so that Alice could potentially receive the *energy that disconfirmed* that she was not worthy of having play partners.

We have to stay alert all the time to provide disconfirming energy when we see our patients activating the neural nets associated with their painful implicit memories. Only when their activation is met by our emotionally alive disconfirmation do the neural nets open to receive what was missing during the hurtful experience. How do we stay present to all the cues, the nonverbal as well as the verbal?

In the next chapter, we are going to talk about mindfulness play and how to repair the errors when we lose our way. We also will explore the importance of mindfulness play in expanding our windows of tolerance and self-regulation.

Chapter 11

MINDFULNESS PLAY

As I prepared to meet 5-year-old Jennifer, I took a few conscious breaths, lengthening the exhalation just a bit to stimulate the ventral vagal parasympathetic (the social engagement system), and then widened my awareness into an open, curious, receptive state. Even though I knew a good deal about her history from her parents and had some left-hemisphere-based idea of what might help mend the attachment wounds she had experienced, my right hemisphere could open to meet her in this moment without an agenda. Even some professionals who practice mindfulness within the cognitive tradition, which is usually known for its goals and interventions, acknowledge that the therapist must let go of desire for change. Randye Semple and Jennifer Lee (2011), authors of *Mindfulness-Based Cognitive Therapy for Anxious Children*, write in their introduction, "The most difficult component of MBCT-C (Mindfulness-Based Cognitive Therapy for Children) for a conventionally trained therapist may be to abandon the desire for change. Letting go of the desire to change may in itself catalyze significant changes" (p. 3). We might call this the first stage of mindfulness—our nonjudgmental acceptance of the child as he or she is when entering the playroom this particular day. I was seeking to silently invite Jennifer to begin based on her internal impulse and wisdom without any interference from an expectation held by me. I knew that whatever she did, she would be telling me the implicit, embodied truth about how she was in that moment—

and that it was important for me to be with her fully in this initial meeting.

How can we trust that the people who come to us can be this self-guided? We might recall that all human brains are complex systems, which means they have the capacity to self-organize and are moving toward integration all the time, unless there are constraints. Even with substantial relational injuries forming significant constraints, the neural nets holding pain and fear can open, in the presence of someone who provides safety through mindful attentiveness, to receive the needed disconfirming energy—which in turn opens the door so that trapped energy and information can join the integrative stream.

Our capacity for mindful attention is the bedrock on which safety for our clients rests. I knew that through her mirror neurons and resonance circuits, Jennifer could sense (probably below conscious awareness) that I was fully with her. I was not seeing her as disordered or defective, but was curious about how she had adapted to the family stress of having a sick older brother from the time she was born. I believed that her behavioral challenges were a meaningful response to those tragic circumstances. Without any words, my non-judgmental and respectful state of mind could touch her inner world and provide some reassurance, while my ventral vagal state was extending an invitation for her to move into relationship whenever she was ready.

During our first two sessions, she moved randomly around the room, picking up objects and setting them down. Coming across the doctor's kit, she began to breathe more quickly and turned away, looking in my direction. Attending mindfully to my own body, I could track the rise in her SNS through an elevation in my own, and then with a little breathing, move back into ventral vagal. Perhaps assisted by resonance with my nervous system, she began to settle as well and then found a big soft blanket to wrap herself in, along with two teddy bears, saying, "One of these bears is sick and the other one isn't." I felt sadness and a little agitation arising in my chest, silently acknowledging and holding these feelings between us. This could be called the second stage of mindfulness when the resonance circuitry that links us with our clients provides the means by which windows of tolerance can begin to expand. As I am able to sense and hold Jennifer's emerging upset within my own window, hers will gradually begin to expand—and actually mine will continue to grow as well. Over many sessions, this process will weave together the neural circuitry of self-regulation as her brain begins to be wired more like mine through resonance. Without technique or intervention, our expanding capacity for mindful presence exerts a powerful influence on the function and even the structure of others' brains.

This capacity for attunement is also the foundation for repairing ruptures. When our social engagement system is on, we are able to read the faces of others and can see when something we have done or said has not been experienced as empathic. One day, as I opened the door to bring Jennifer into the playroom, my face assumed its usual delighted smile. Instead, I found her mother there, looking distraught. As she caught sight of my smiling face, I could tell it wounded her because it didn't meet her where she was. I felt the pain of that immediately and my face quickly took on the feeling of concern that welled up in me. Such ongoing ruptures with the potential for repair are the stuff of being human. The more we cultivate a mindful, socially engaged presence, the greater the likelihood that we will be able to make these all-important repairs—which are the very foundation of secure relationships and resilience.

We may begin to sense that developing our own mindfulness practice can be a significant aid to being more fully and nonjudgmentally present to our clients and also to ourselves. A mindfulness practice may also provide protection against burnout by leaving us in a less anxious, more attuned, more self-accepting state of mind. Research across a number of different studies has shown improvement in immune functioning and cardiac health as well as decreases in symptoms of anxiety and depression, to name just a few of the benefits of mindfulness-based practices (Baer (2006); Baer, Smith, Hopkins, Krietemeyer, & Toney, 2006). Studies (Lazar et al., 2005) also show a correlation between insight meditation and the thickening of the middle prefrontal cortex (important in response flexibility and emotional modulation) and the right anterior insula (relay station between body and cortex). There is probably no better practice to widen our own window of tolerance for intense emotion.

Becoming familiar with mindfulness practices also paves the way for the third stage of mindfulness: teaching more formal practices to those with whom we work, whether they be parents, children, or the adults who come to us to play. As an aid to being more mindfully aware of what is going on in our bodies and brains, I often teach patients about some of the basic structure and function of key brain circuits—in a playful way. Borrowing Siegel's (2012) hand model of the brain, I ask children and even parents to use face paints on their hands to explore the circuitry (Figure 11.1).

We paint the heart and lungs on the base of the palm to represent the functions that our brain stem helps us regulate. Then we paint feelings on our thumbs and in the palm of our hands for the limbic system, and then discover something to represent the thinking and relating part of our prefrontal cortex on our knuckles. Some children get creative and paint spinal cords on their wrists or eyes on their fingernails. Then we play with "flipping our lids" as we open and close our fingers over our thumbs, simulating the movement in and out of dysregulation. Children especially love doing this exercise with their parents. Sometimes they paint each other's hands, and

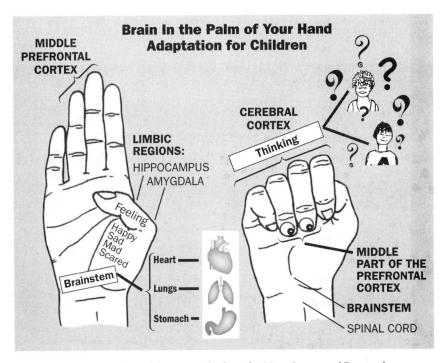

FIGURE 11.1. Adapted from *Mindsight: The New Science of Personal Transformation*, by Daniel J. Siegel, M.D. (2012), p.15.

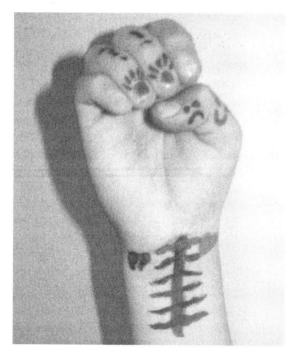

Photo of Child's Hand: Photo courtesy of the author. Used with permission.

then I ask them to take turns explaining what their hand drawings mean. From then on, I can just show them the palm of my hand to bring up the colorful image of the "brain in the palm of our hands."

With this information about how brains work embodied in their hands, children and adults begin to become more mindfully aware when they feel dysregulation coming on, and they are more consciously able to change direction rather than follow the old, well-worn paths. When Jennifer felt sad, she would sometimes paint her thumb blue and just show it to her mother, who had now learned to just hold her quietly until the grief they both felt became less simply because they were connected to one another.

There are also numerous practices that can be offered to children and parents to increase their capacity for mindful awareness and attunement. The Mindful Awareness Research Center at University of California at Los Angeles (www.marc.ucla.edu) has many recorded meditations available online, an especially useful resource for parents. Susan Kaiser Greenland (2010) has developed a program to nurture kids in mindfulness from a very young age (www.susankaiser greenland.com/inner-kids-program.html). Her program stresses inner awareness, outer awareness, and blending the two without losing either one, leading to attention, balance, and compassion—what she calls "The New ABCs." One aspect to keep in mind is that teaching children mindfulness skills differs greatly from teaching adults. Sample, Lee, and Miller (2006) draw attention to developmental issues that require some creative adaptations. They say, humorously, "We found that adults rarely (if ever) use their meditation mats to construct forts, and in our experience, never experiment to see how many meditation cushions they can balance on their heads" (p. 143). Recognizing that children are not just little adults, they offer suggestions for teaching children mindfulness skills. Building on these, Semple and Lee (2011) wrote an entire manual for treating childhood anxiety based on mindfulness-based cognitive therapy for children (MBCT-C). The resources are rich and varied.

One particular kind of mindfulness practice seems to nurture compassion and calmness at the same time. At times of upset, placing one hand on the heart and one on the belly, and sending messages of kindness and comfort inside, can sometimes provide almost instantaneous relief. We have a brain in our heart and one in our belly, as well as the one in the skull. The belly brain reports on how safe we feel, and the heart brain gives us messages about how connected we are. Making direct contact with the area nearest these brains seems to provide reassurance that we are attending to these messages and that there is a compassionate part of ourselves that is not caught up in the upset.

Because of the ongoing suffering in Jennifer's household as her brother's condition worsened, there was a great need for comfort. I taught this young one and her mother about the two brains, and we practiced together. We would first find the place that felt just right for our hands on our chests and bellies for sending these messages, and then picture the sadness and fear that needed our help. Together, we would discover the words that this sadness and fear needed and silently send them inward. With just a little practice, the tension and grief would melt from their faces to a significant degree. Mom said she could feel her belly relax from its ongoing clenched state, and Jennifer often felt warmth that went all the way through her chest from front to back. As relaxation increased, tears would often flow—and we came to understand that these were necessary and right and healing.

As we conclude this brief but important visit with mindfulness in the playroom, let's spend a little time again with the central paradox: that therapy usually involves presenting problems, treatment plans, and session goals, all requiring objectivity and good judgment on the part of the therapist. If we approach someone with an agenda of change, however, we have assumed a defectiveness model. As we saw with Alice in the last chapter, genuine change emerges when patients feel the deep acceptance that allows them to open the dissociated neural nets of terror, pain, or abandonment that they have carried as implicit memories. We all hold these kinds of memories in implicit form to protect our emotional and psychological integrity, and only when we have a neuroception of safety can we bring them into the light of day. The synapses of these neural nets are unlocked, not because someone wants to help us change, but because we believe that we are accepted and loved as we are.

We can hold the paradox—the intentional therapeutic goals of a treatment plan *and* the willingness to let go of the need to change something—if we remember that our divided brain is capable of dual processing. Because our left and right hemispheres process simultaneously, often collaborating, and sometimes inhibiting each other, we can manage the paradox by holding the therapeutic goals with the left hemisphere while we open as fully as we can to this particular moment—something that only happens in the right hemisphere —where change becomes possible when we create a space for the wisdom within the child to guide us. For the most part, if we have done our "homework" (taking good histories and working out of a science-informed base), we can trust that our left hemispheres will not fail in their duties to hold the therapeutic structure that supports the intuitive decision-making processes of our right hemispheres.

Higgins-Klein (2013) writes about the stillness that is so important as we hold the complexity of our therapeutic relationships. She says, "Healing occurs when the therapist and child together descend into their respective places of inner stillness" (p. xxii). We can support our patients moving through life's difficult experiences when they are with us as we hold their concerns mindfully. We accept them as they are, we link with them as we help them expand their windows of tolerance, and we teach them skills that they can use when they are not with us.

I often think about the children, the families, and the adults who have come to me for therapy. I also think about the many school children we worked with in our sand tray project. I wonder if they are still playing in ways that support their development and creativity. And I am always wondering how we can broaden what we know about the healing power of mindfulness play—teaching people the "how to" of relational play. In a way, it seems quite strange to think about teaching anyone to play since the motivational PLAY system is something we inherit at birth. It would seem that play should happen naturally. We look at puppies, kittens, and bear cubs, and we can see that play is almost impossible to stop. Even decorticated rats will play at every opportunity—and sometimes even more vigorously than rats with fully intact brains (Panksepp, 1998).

Somehow we grown-up humans have more difficulty allowing this natural play. We have become so serious, and it seems we have relegated play to a nonproductive status—a child's waste of time. In our concluding chapter we are going to consider possible explanations for the changing status of play in human cultures and what it might mean for our future well-being.

PART III

Collaborating with Parents, Teachers, and Colleagues

Chapter 12

WHEN DID WE STOP PLAYING AND HOW DO WE BEGIN AGAIN?

Mrs. Weston called to make an appointment for her twin boys, Jacob and Joshua. I knew the family well because I had treated the boys when the Westons first took them in as foster children. Jacob and Joshua were 6 years old then, and by the time they came to the Weston family, they had experienced moving into and out of multiple foster homes. Trauma and abandonment had become the reality of what was *normal* to them. I worked intensely with the family for 2 years. We did family play sessions, family talk sessions, individual play sessions for each boy, and sometimes sibling play. The work–play was challenging for all of us, but rewarding to the point that Mr. and Mrs. Weston decided to adopt the boys when they were 8 years old. At that point, we began decreasing the frequency of the therapy sessions, and by the time they were 9 years old, we were meeting about once a month just to help them consolidate their gains. These monthly sessions were quite delightful for me because I could see that the family had learned to play together, and that it was helping them deepen and maintain their family bonds. Soon after Joshua and Jacob celebrated their 10th birthdays, I recommended that we transition into therapy *as needed*. We decided to do a family sand tray to mark the completion of the therapy.

Before we began the tray, we reviewed briefly all they had been through and had accomplished. Mr. and Mrs. Weston made it clear to Joshua and Jacob that this session was really just an important milestone in their family journey, and that if things should come up in the future, more therapy sessions would be possible. They made a sand tray, and I was deeply moved by how much fun they had playing together, collaborating, and working out the details of what they needed in their world. They chose to use my 4-foot round tray to make a village that included lots of people, animals, trees, gardens, and spiritual symbols. Joshua asked his mother to help him pick out all the blue gems, so that he could make a stream running through the world. Jacob and his father created a fishing scene with a small boy and his father casting their lines in the stream. Mrs. Weston was an artist, and her influence was quite visible in their creation. The tray was aesthetically beautiful, and I could tell that they were pleased with themselves.

When Mrs. Weston called me on the telephone to make this new appointment, it had been 4 years since the family celebration tray, and she reminded me that the boys were now 14 years old. She said that Joshua's academic work was deteriorating rapidly, and that Jacob was getting into lots of trouble. His most recent infraction had involved ditching school. I asked her if anything in particular had happened that might explain their changing behaviors. She said that she and her husband were experiencing some financial stress, but she couldn't think of anything that might be affecting the boys. I asked to meet with the parents before meeting the boys so that I could catch up on what had happened over the last 4 years.

When we met, I could tell that Mr. Weston was experiencing a great deal of stress related to his new construction business. When he first started his company, it had gone extremely well, but just after he had signed contracts to expand his business, the economy went into a serious recession. He was now on the verge of losing his enterprise. Prior to this, the Westons had enjoyed financial security, allowing them to provide their boys with ample opportunities for recreational activities and fun vacations, so there had been considerable change in the family lifestyle recently.

I had a hunch that the boys were experiencing vicarious stress, so I decided to talk with the parents about Porges's (2011) hierarchy of arousal zones (see Chapter 2). I wanted to help them understand that the financial stress might be triggering old implicit memories of trauma and abandonment in Joshua and Jacob. I explained to them that when we move out of the safe zone of the social engagement system, our cognitive resources diminish as we put energy into protecting ourselves from danger. I speculated that perhaps Jacob's ditching school might be a flight response, and Joshua could be experiencing some hypoarousal (freeze) with his academic deterioration. Mr. Weston suddenly said, "That's me! That is exactly what is happening to me." He then went into some detail about sleepless nights and the lack of focus at work. He understood the cognitive impairment, and from this discussion, he became empathic not only for his sons, but also for himself.

I talked with Mr. and Mrs. Weston about how play helps children and adults widen their windows of tolerance, thus improving self-regulation. It suddenly occurred to both of them that they had not been playing together as a family. Mrs. Weston said, "When did we stop playing?" They realized that it was about the time the financial setback happened. I also asked them if their sons knew what was happening to the family business. They said they had not talked about it because they were trying to protect the boys from worrying. As we continued to talk, they began to see that their strategy had not worked. We scheduled a family session.

The following week when they arrived, I was surprised to see how tall both boys had grown, and equally surprised by their reluctance to talk. Jacob, fidgeting and avoiding eye contact, appeared to be agitated, while Joshua, head down, acknowledged in an almost inaudible voice that his parents were unhappy with his grades. Jacob seemed to want distance, signaling that he wanted to be left alone, and Joshua looked depressed. Although I have never done therapy out of a defectiveness model, both boys were acting as if I were seeing them as defective. We had to set that straight, and so we began by talking with them about what was happening to the family finances. They already knew that money was tight because recreational activities had been seriously curtailed. I asked them what they understood about the money situation. Jacob said, "It's like when you're homeless, and you don't have a place to live." Clearly the "unspoken financial stress" was triggering his implicit memories. I could see the expression of surprise on his mother's face and concern in the father's. Joshua said nothing.

In terms they could understand, I explained to Jacob and Joshua what happens when our nervous systems experience stress. When they had been in therapy before, I had taught them about the brain in the palm of your hand, and we had used face paints to create images of it. I reminded them of that model, and I could see their bodies relax as we talked about how well their bodies were protecting them during such a scary time. As they began to unwind a bit, I decided to offer a family play activity. Joshua and Jacob were now teenagers, and I had a hunch they would not want to resume their earlier childhood patterns of play therapy. I brought out a container of Lego® toys, and said, "I want us to do a family project." Since I was asking their mother and father to join, I did not think the boys would object to playing with these toys even though they were teenagers. One of the reasons I picked the Legos to design a family play activity was because of something I found on the Internet when I first began writing this book and researching what the field of neuroscience was saying about play and play attitudes. One of the things that popped up was the use of Lego Serious Play® (LSP) in corporate and government settings to help adults come up with creative solutions to serious problems. I was intrigued and thought an adaptation of it might work with the Weston family.

SERIOUS LEGO PLAY—SERIOUSLY?

I couldn't help laughing about the idea of connecting the words *serious* and *play* in the same phrase. At the same time, it also made perfect sense to me to modify *play* with the word *serious* in terms of the challenge of trying to get adults, especially in corporate and government institutions, to see the value of play for problem solving (and no doubt for increased productivity). I also could see the potential for adapting LSP for family play therapy whereby adults, adolescents and children could come together in the context of a familiar play system to work on family problems. Like sand tray therapy, LSP integrated several variables (the hand–mind connection, metaphorical thinking, and storytelling), making it attractive for me to offer it to the Weston family in terms of good brain-building interventions for mental integration and well-being.

Of course, we have to wonder, if LSP is a means to some end, is it really play? In terms of the definition of play used by most play scholars who incorporate the idea that play is an activity done for its own sake without concern for outcomes, what could this serious Lego play be? And if it were *serious*, could anyone really be *serious* that it was also *play*? If it could help adults find creative solutions to serious problems, wouldn't it make sense to invite the Weston family to play with the Lego bricks to explore what was happening in their family? Just for the sake of curiosity, I temporarily set aside the usual definition of play (just for fun) to look at how Lego play helps *serious* adults solve problems. Here is what I found.

The Lego Group began in Billund, Denmark in the workshop of a humble carpenter named Ole Kirk Christiansen, who began making wooden toys in 1932 and shortly after named his company *Lego* from the Danish phrase *leg godt*, which means "play well." Only later did he learn that the Latin meaning of *lego* was "I assemble." For decades the Lego company provided a play system based on a limited number of Lego bricks to help children "build their own dreams," thus, envisioning their own futures. Around 1998, when the Lego company was facing near bankruptcy, Lego Serious Play® was born in an attempt to unlock innovative solutions within the company. They took to heart what they had been telling children all along: "Play well" with the bricks and "assemble" your vision of who you are and who you can become. LSP went through a number of iterations from 1998 to 2010, building on the assumption that the answers to problems are "already in the room" if you can access the collective intelligence of the group by inviting participants to "think with their hands." In the case of the Weston family, I wanted to put the tools of play in their hands to help them access their core resilience to solve family problems. Specifically, they needed to restore their social engagement system as a family (Porges, 2011).

As the Weston boys began to eagerly engage with the Lego toys, I was reminded of that well-used quote by Carl Jung, "Often the hands know how to solve a riddle with which the intellect has wrestled in vain" (Jung, 1969, par. 180—CW 8:180). Knowing now about the distribution of neurons throughout the body, and that each hand is connected to the opposite side of the brain (left hand to right hemisphere, and right hand to left hemisphere), we can imagine already the benefit of the Westons using both hands (and both sides of the brain) simultaneously to "think" or "play" through the issues at hand. It was clear to me that an adaptation of LSP offered the elements that were necessary for family problem solving in the context of play therapy, and I believed strongly that it could help the Weston family heal from the stress induced by economic difficulties. From an integrated neuroscience and play therapy perspective, I could see the potential use of systematic Lego play with families based on the following principles:

1. Thinking with the body (hand–mind connection during Lego model building) is now well supported by neuroscience.
2. Nurturing the right–left–right progression (McGilchrist, 2009)—beginning in the right hemisphere (model building), moving to the left hemisphere (storytelling), and returning back to the right hemisphere (metaphorical understanding at a higher level)—supports meaningful and creative brain processes.
3. Accessing the family (group) intelligence on a level playing field where every member creates a model and tells a story maximizes group problem solving because each participant, regardless of age or rank, is valued equally for his or her unique contribution.
4. Enhancing neuroception of safety through a limited set of materials that each person can easily master invites the motivational SEEKING, PLAY, and CARE systems to become active in the spirit of we are "just playing," thus strengthening family relationships in the safe zone of play (Porges, 2011).

As we have discussed earlier in this book, the activation of these subcortical motivational systems (in this case, SEEKING, PLAY, and CARE) powerfully influences decisions and behaviors that are regulated in higher brain regions. The subcortical is evident in the cortical processes, just as the cortical processes influence the subcortical reminding us once again of Panksepp's (2011) nested BrainMind hierarchies (see Chapter 3).

I love the LSP idea of "thinking with your fingers," and it fit with my understanding of one of the ways sand tray therapy has been so useful in the play therapy room with both children and adults. Although the LSP method is a little more directive than what I usually do with the sand tray method, it still combines the hand–mind connection, metaphorical thinking, and storytelling to foster integrated brain processes. In LSP each participant uses Lego bricks (including metaphorical pieces) to discover and construct his or her ideas about a particular issue that a trained facilitator presents to the group. This building phase occurs before anyone has said a word about how to resolve the problem at stake, giving everyone equal standing as they set their own point of view on the table (literally and metaphorically). An open-source document describes the reason why LSP facilitators ask participants to make things with their hands rather than just talking.

> Research has shown that the process of making something, which is then discussed, can lead to much more valuable, insightful and honest discussions. . . . The creative, reflective process of making something prompts the brain to work in a different way, and can unlock new perspectives. . . .
>
> When we give shape and form to our imagination, by constructing and externalizing concepts—making them tangible and shareable—we can not only reflect on them ourselves, but invite others to reflect with us. LEGO® SERIOUS PLAY® offers an engaging hands-on environment, where the activity is perceived as meaningful, one's abilities are in balance with the challenge at hand, and one has the tools to express the emerging knowledge. . . .
>
> It does not set any path for the individual or group to follow, but rather embraces and supports any ideas that may emerge, and encourages development and collaboration to make these stronger. Every stage of the LEGO® SERIOUS PLAY® process involves building with LEGO bricks, utilizing the "hand–mind connection": there is never a point where participants merely sit back and write down, or chat about, the issues without building their response first. Therefore everything that is discussed comes from out of the building process, where the hand and mind engage to give visual, metaphorical shape to meaningful things, emotions, and relationships.
>
> The idea that we need to "think with the body" has gained support from a convergence of new evidence from psychology and neuroscience. These theories emphasize that cognitive processes such as learning and memory are strongly influenced by the way we use our bodies to interact with the physical world. (http://seriousplaypro.com/about/about-serious-play/lsp-open-source/)

In this description the word *emerging* appears several times; emergence is the hallmark of connection with right-mode processing, which attends to what is happening in this moment, within the emerging flow of new experience. When added to our already active left mode, this is the zone of creativity. Whether we are dealing with work issues or family struggles, putting the right mode in the lead and allowing what has not yet been thought to emerge through our hands gives our naturally integrating brains the opportunity to bring forth something never before imagined. Contact with the right also includes the emotional and relational along with the more left-based strategic way of thinking, creating a more complete picture. I imagine that the SEEKING system becomes quite active as we move away from the words-only environment of the left and enter this zone of safe PLAY.

FAMILY LEGO PLAY

David Gauntlett (2007) suggests that the concept of play for purposes of LSP may work best when it is thought of as a "fruitful metaphor for thinking freely and without constraints, a state where one is happy to try different things knowing that there is no right or wrong answer" (p. 134). This attitude keeps us from getting stuck in the left-hemisphere "unpacking" processes where linear and logical thinking are so dominant. The systematic model building of Lego play applied to family therapy helps to ensure that the family does not get stuck in old and rigid patterns of left-hemisphere thinking.

We know from Panksepp's (1998: Panksepp & Biven, 2012) laboratory work that the primary motivation system of PLAY is rooted in subcortical regions of the brain. At that level, parents and children share a joint system. As our brains develop, the primary urge to play is woven into the higher levels of the brain in secondary and tertiary processes, as we saw in Chapter 3, thus allowing the metaphorical process, at varying levels of sophistication, to appeal to both children and adults. Most parents, however, have the cognitive resources and sophistication to appreciate how metaphorical thinking works, and even though most children just enjoy swimming in the metaphors, parents often appreciate how the model of building–playing enhances family connections. When the PLAY system is accessed, whether in parents or children, it can profoundly influence cognitive processes. The application of LSP to family therapy is not only an effective way to help parents access unique information from within, enhancing creativity and productivity while having fun, it also shows us once again that play is a core developmental process across the lifespan—from the babies who play with their mothering people to the play that happens in our therapy offices with children, teens, and parents.

CHANGING ATTITUDES TOWARD PLAY

In our Western cultures it seems to me that we somehow have lost the vision of the benefits and possibility of play across the lifespan, at home, at school, or even in the workplace. Historically, we have seen play as the province of children, and we have held benign attitudes of tolerance toward children playing, but in more recent years, it appears that, even with our children, we have gone from tolerance to a more restrictive stance. Most adults are generally uneasy with rough-and-tumble play, and the pressures of a world that seems to be speeding up leaves little time for the leisure of exploratory play in families or with peer groups. Worse, we have begun to eliminate play from most school environments, where recess is disappearing for fear of liability for injuries and of children being "left behind" academically if they play too much. We seem to have adopted the idea (without any evidence base) that we can help children learn better by taking away the extracurricular activities at school—music, art, drama, and play.

It was not always this way. Jeremy Rifkin (2000) believes that the coming of the Industrial Age was a turning point in our attitudes toward play. He explains:

> Anthropologists, however, remind us that from the beginning of human existence until the Industrial Age, human beings spent far more time playing than working. In the Medieval Age, for example, nearly half the days of the Christian calendrical year were holidays, feast days, or days of rest. When the French Republic issued a decree replacing the Christian calendar with a secular one containing far fewer holidays, the peasant class revolted, forcing the government to rescind its order. Only in the Industrial Age did work come to dominate human affairs and play recede to the background. (p. 261)

171

Given what we now know about play, do we really want to rele-
gate it to the background? Application of LSP to family therapy is a
good demonstration of the power of play to access creative and
deeply felt ideas, and it may give us pause about our society's attitudes toward play. Rifkin (2000) cites the Dutch historian Johan
Huizinga as one of the first to talk about the importance of play in
the making of a society. He argued that all cultures arise in play: "It
is through this playing that society expresses its interpretation of life
and the world" (Huizinga, 1955, p. ix). Rifkin goes on to say, "All of
the critical activities of human society—language, myth, ritual, folk-
lore, philosophy, dance, music, theater, law, even the rules of war-
fare—are born of play" (Rifkin, 2000, p. 261). When I first read these
words, I liked them, but I thought they were perhaps overstated.
Having come through the journey of writing this book about play,
however, especially learning about the LSP project, I no longer think
it is an overvaluation of play. I can see how the culture of a healthy
family, arising through play, contributes to the culture as a whole the
creative energy necessary for its evolution.

HOW DO WE TALK TO A LEFT HEMISPHERE
THAT DEVALUES PLAY?

When I teach therapists how to use the sand tray method, I ask them
to build something with their hands—a world imagined by their
deeper mind and built entirely of miniatures nestled, buried, or resting in the sand. We start with that activity so that they can experience what it is like to be open to the surprises that arise when we
allow our right-mode processes to take the lead. Being able to draw
from this foundational bodily experience, I find that it is easier to
teach difficult neuroscience concepts, and I believe it is easier for
the therapists to learn as well because they can make sense of the
abstract concepts by encountering them as bodily experiences. McGilchrist (2009) says this right-mode perspective is where we live our
actual lives. Whether I am with an individual client or teaching a
group of therapists, I have learned how important it is to allow time
for full immersion in the right-hemisphere experiential process. When
we give the right hemisphere a chance to experience fully, the bridg-
ing to the left hemisphere is very natural. In the left hemisphere, the

right hemisphere experiences are "unpacked" (to use McGilchrist's word), using narrative and analytical processes to deepen conscious understanding. The left hemisphere loves to tell stories about what the right experiences. In the absence of experience, the left hemisphere has no story to tell—at least, not an authentic one.

I first became aware of how important metaphorical thinking is through my experiences with the sand tray methodology, but it has become clear to me over the years that almost any kind of play has the potential for this same *bodily grounding* in the right hemisphere and *unpacking* in the left, if we choose to collaborate with the natural processes of the brain as it moves in its right–left–right progression as McGilchrist (2009) describes it (see Chapter 9, Figure 9.1).

The biggest challenge for me has been finding ways to get therapists to try the play that allows them to access their right hemispheres. So often they have told me that they came to learn about the sand tray with great skepticism, only because a colleague told them they should try it. One tray is often enough to open a new appreciation for what the voice of the right has to share. After they have had this experience, they are much more able to support sand tray with children and their parents in the playroom. Having had an embodied experience of the power of sand and miniatures, they carry a different sense of conviction about its value in opening the deeper implicit places that are largely without language. Their conviction becomes an invisible encouragement to their clients to partake as well.

Even with extensive training in play therapy, we can still find it hard as adults to deeply value play, given the cultural ethos against it. We have been told in so many subtle and not-so-subtle ways that we need to get serious if we expect to accomplish anything. We are asked to set play aside and study hard—even in many of the graduate schools that educate therapists who work with children and families. We are initiated in the ways of the left hemisphere, sometimes to the exclusion of the right. It is easy to get stuck there for all the reasons McGilchrist (2009) cites: There is predictive power in the left hemisphere; it gives us a pseudo-sense of security in a sometimes overwhelming world, insulating us somewhat from the suffering that is going on around us and helping us focus so that we can find the one single grain of corn in the field of gravel. There is nothing wrong with this focus, but when it becomes the only focus, we simply forget how to live and relate with one another. If Huizinga (1955) is right, we might even lose our human way of creating a culture in which any of us would want to live.

Panksepp's (1998, 2010, Panksepp & Biven, 2012) work has made it abundantly clear that we are born with the primal urge to play. In a left-dominant culture, we are cut off from most of our moment-to-moment experiences, so play, which is the essence of being in the joyful moment, has been devalued, thwarted, and even discarded. It also may be that the dominance of isolated left-hemisphere thinking, with its powerful means for controlling the environment, might create a painful and harmful imbalance in our core biological systems that have designed our brains for the dynamic of a right–left–right progression grounded in metaphorical thinking.

Evidence-Based *or* Science-Informed

Thinking about how we have approached the use of play in the mental health field, and also thinking about McGilchrist's (2009) notion of the divided brain, I am wondering if part of the problem in our society's devaluation of play lies in how we have chosen to apply the scientific method to our field. Eager to be respected as a part of behavioral science, it seems that we have adopted the "evidence-based" terminology of a left-hemisphere perspective. Our mental health facilities, family agencies, and school counseling programs all require scientific "evidence" that the treatment methods have been proven effective for helping people change behaviors. Unfortunately, this grasping for "evidence" may have created a left-hemisphere imbalance in how we do our science, blinding us to the crucial need to include aspects that aren't easily measured: the power of relationship to heal, the capacity of play to let us be in touch with aspects of experience that language can't reach, and the resources of the right hemisphere in discovering new ways of being and behaving in the midst of the freedom of play.

We know that the left hemisphere, left on its own, without connection to the right, is capable of confabulating—of just making things up. There can be no true science with a *left hemisphere only* perspective. We now have a wealth of scientific information about how the right hemisphere works (due partially to the ability of the left hemisphere to tease out the facts). We do know that the *right hemisphere alone* is responsible for receiving new information from the environment. We also know that it is relational, integrative, emotional, and playful—all the things that make life worthwhile and potentially joyful. To me it seems tragic that we may be disregarding the depth of this science just because it does not fit a left-hemisphere perspective.

A recent issue of the *American Journal of Play*, devoted entirely to challenges associated with the scientific research of play, underscores the problems associated with bias toward experimental research in laboratory-type settings. In response to a critical review of play research by Lillard et al (2013), a number of authors address this problem in thoughtful and comprehensive ways. Two of the articles, considering the relationship between play and the development of children's self-regulation and executive function capabilities, are particularly relevant in the context of this book. One addresses the role of make-believe play in the development of executive functioning (Berk & Meyers, 2013), and the other draws from the theories of Vygotsky to discuss play and self-regulation (Bodrova, Germeroth, & Leong, 2013).

Remembering what McGilchrist (2009) said about the example of a bird looking for a single grain of corn in the gravel field and how it also needed its other hemisphere to keep track of the whole environment, lest it become someone else's lunch, I think it would make a big difference if we could change our language a little in terms of deciding about the legitimacy of our mental health treatments. Instead of using only the term *evidence-based*, we could say, *evidence-based* or *science-informed*. With that kind of terminology, we would still be honoring and relying on our scientific method, while simultaneously opening up to those *promising practices* that are emerging out of a rapidly developing field of neuroscience.

The Nervous System's Dilemma

Although the fields of education and mental health pride themselves on being grounded in evidence-based practices, glaring exceptions sometimes occur. The recess debate is one good example. Despite ample research evidence that recess is essential for children to maintain their mental and emotional balance (not to mention that it also improves children's cognitive abilities, helping them to focus better and to retain information) (Pellegrini, 2005, 2008; Pellegrini & Bohn-Gettler, 2013; Ramstetter, Murray, & Garner, 2010), there has been a trend since the 1990s to reduce and sometimes even eliminate recess on school playgrounds. Even more puzzling, some of the newer schools have been built *without* playgrounds. Our nation's fear of falling behind in academics on the world stage seems to be the primary reason for reducing playtime at school, something that clearly harms the mental health of children, while short-circuiting their ability to learn (Gray, 2011). Panksepp (2007, 2008) believes that the attention-deficit/hyperactivity disorder (ADHD) epidemic we appear to have may be due, in part, to the lack of play. Based on his scientific studies, he actually recommends beginning the school day with recess so that the motivational need to play is satisfied, thus allowing better concentration on schoolwork and at the same time, giving our children the space and support to develop their relational capacity, a key component in ongoing mental health.

It may be that this environment of fear permeating our schools, making human connection difficult and undermining our capacity to make changes, lies at the heart of this dilemma. A frightened nervous system can't access the circuitry of play or take in new ideas, particularly when it will take a great deal of effort to manifest something new. We face the same challenge in our playrooms. As hurting parents bring their struggling children to me, they often have the same culturally influenced question: "How can play possibly help my child behave better and do better at school?"

Choosing Play Consciously

How might we find our way out of these pervasive difficulties? The left hemisphere cannot really know what the right hemisphere knows (and experiences) when we play. The very fact that it is almost impossible for play scholars to agree on a definition of play makes it difficult for researchers using a left-hemisphere-only perspective to measure exactly what happens when we play. Science informs us, however, that we do need to be in our ventral vagal parasympathetic system (the social engagement system) to play with one another. When this circuit slows the heart (the vagal brake), our fight–flight–freeze responses decrease, thereby reducing the stress hormone cortisol (Porges, 2011). Marc Otto (2010), a play specialist, speaks beautifully about what he has learned from children concerning interactive physical play:

> Through becoming familiar with play at the hands and hearts of thousands and thousands of children, I have learned that in any moment I have a choice—to fight, flee or freeze, or to flow into connection. Such is the gift of play.
>
> Becoming familiar with PLAY means nothing less than embracing the tenderness of our heart, the fullness of our mind, and the softness of our belly in all moments. And remembering that we are here to be family. (p. 75)

Making this conscious choice to flow into connection may be the most important lesson that we can learn from play. In the play therapy room, our need for safety and human connection is at the root of all we do. If we can remember that neural change is supported when we are in safe connection with others, it will be much easier for us to make the conscious choice of staying in our ventral vagal heartfelt place of relating. Play, or even a playful attitude toward our work, helps us move into and stay in that place of connection where optimal learning and therapeutic healing can take place.

It is difficult for a left-hemisphere-only perspective to embrace the idea that the emotional–motivational circuits of PLAY and CARE might be crucial to learning. Despite the left hemisphere's inability to experience what the right hemisphere knows, if we understand that our divided brains evolved for a reason, and not just as an error on the part of Mother Nature, we can make conscious choices to trust our right hemisphere's ability to see and feel the larger picture. We can consciously invite the integration that McGilchrist (2009) helps us visualize in his image of the right–left–right progression (see Chapter 9, Figure 9.1). When I think about that image, I can envision a *spiral of play* whereby we embody our experiences in the world through playing: anticipating, wondering, being surprised, discovering, shifting our perspectives, taking in new sensations, laughing, and feeling the pleasures of encountering the unexpected. These play experiences come in through our right hemispheres and are mapped there, grounding them as our view of the world metaphorically in that moment. As these embodied experiences move into the left hemisphere, understanding comes, and we acquire new knowledge or new understanding of how the world works as our experiences are "unpacked" by the left hemisphere through analyzing, synthesizing, and integrating ideas. Our willingness to allow this dynamic collaboration and integration of both sides of our brains results in new levels of mastery and empowerment. The spiral automatically moves us back to the metaphorical understanding of the right hemisphere, only now we are a little higher (or a little more developed), and we are ready to begin a new cycle of play from this new level of understanding.

The spiral fits for me because it is an image of continuous circular flow that embraces both hemispheres in ever-increasing complexity. As McGilchrist (2009) suggests, if the two hemispheres collaborate in this dynamic relationship, "they are invincible" (p. 428), but if not, the left hemisphere is capable of usurping the power of the right to the detriment and suffering of both.

Rifkin (2000) points to a similar kind of imbalance in the place where play encounters the sphere of economics. He thinks that we are actually in danger of "commodifying" play: packaging it in ways that make it marketable in what he believes is the new economy of cultural capitalism (following industrial capitalism). He describes a situation where all of life could become a "paid-for" experience with themed cities, entertainment destination centers, sports and games, virtual worlds, movies, television, and so on. This would be in contrast to what he calls "mature play" that always occurs in the cultural arena where connection is core. He explains: "Mature play brings people together into shared community. It is both the most intimate and the most sophisticated form of human communication that exists. Mature play is also the antidote to the unbridled exercise of institutional power, be it political or commercial in nature" (p. 265).

Rifkin also describes "pure play" as "the highest expression of human freedom," pointing to the fact that freedom cannot be purchased. He quotes Friedrich Schiller (1795), who said: "Man plays only when he is in the fullest sense of the word a human being, and he is fully a human being only when he plays" (as cited in Rifkin, 2000, p. 264). Rifkin believes that pure play in the cultural realm is the supreme expression of human bonding. He says:

We play with one another out of love of human communication. It is the deepest act of participation between people and is made possible by a collective trust—the feeling that each player can let down his defenses and abandon himself, for the moment, to the care of others so he can experience the joy that comes from a communion. One can't truly play alone for the same reason one can't truly experience joy in isolation. Both are shared experiences.

Freedom and play, then, share a common ground. It is through the experience of pure play in the cultural sphere that one learns to participate openly with one's fellow human beings. We become truly human by reveling in one another. Human beings can never be really free until we are able to fully enter into pure play. (2000, p. 264)

When we look at play this way, seeing it as having a common ground with freedom, none of us can take lightly the devaluing of play in our society. Personally, I feel sad knowing that many children are growing up in neighborhoods considered by parents to be unsafe for the free exploratory play that I enjoyed as a child. My grandchildren have a hard time imagining how I could have grown up without a television or ever having visited Disneyland. It's true! We did, however, have a natural "play sanctuary," the kind Plato talked about, where we were free to make up our own play activities, and I think we were lucky. My brothers and sisters and I lived in a small town where we could play outside with other neighborhood children free from fear. My parents did not have to worry about where we were because we were safe in a neighborhood where we never had to lock our doors.

I am deeply grateful for having had ample opportunities for safe play. Even so, I would not want to return to the "good old days," even if we could. There is something quite rich in the current variety of playful activities we have created (and commodified) for our children. I love taking my grandson to Explora, a wonderful children's museum, where we can experience many different play activities all in an afternoon's time. At the same time, I am concerned, as is Rifkin, about the commodification of play. It is hard for me to imagine that my grandchildren and their children might be moving into an era where most of play would be "paid-for" structured experiences. If that were to happen, I think we could lose play as an avenue to our emotional well-being, and perhaps, as Rifkin suggests, to our very way of life.

BEGINNING AGAIN

Despite the dangers of over commodifying play, I don't think it is possible to go back. I believe we need to find our way through our dilemma of knowing from science that play is essential to our well-being, yet being too fearful that we are falling behind somehow, and that play would be the easiest thing to sacrifice so that we could have more time to achieve whatever it is that we are trying to achieve. From a *left-hemisphere-only* position, the commodification of material things (including play activities) seems like a natural solution. The left hemisphere is skilled at and comfortable with packaging things in known quantities—things that can be measured and tested and are therefore predictable. And Rifkin would add, in the new economy of cultural capitalism, these things can be sold.

How do we move through this dilemma? We can begin from a science-informed perspective that tells us that we have good reason to let go of fear about the demise of play. We know the circuitry of play is inborn, and we can easily observe that whenever it is given even a little chance, the predisposition to play will manifest. Panksepp (2007) would say, even without being given a chance, it will emerge, as it sometimes does in the form of ADHD with play-deprived children. There is no dispute about the biological basis of play.

Science also informs us that play has a relational core that prepares us to live in an unpredictable world (Panksepp & Biven, 2012; Pellis & Pellis, 2009; Pellis, Pellis & Bell, 2010; Brown & Vaughn, 2009). The development of motor, cognitive, social, and emotional skills are often on the list of reasons why play scholars believe we have dedicated play circuits in the brain. Pellis and Pellis (2009) suggest, however, that *emotional calibration* is the primary avenue for the improvement of the motor, cognitive, and social skills. They say, "A fearful and anxious animal is not one that is fully capable of bringing to bear, in any given situation, all its motor and cognitive skills" (p. 162). They believe that this *emotional calibration*—knowing how far you can press another, when you should back off, and how to manage your emotions—is the primary purpose of play, and that it is this skill that most allows us to deal with an unpredictable world. Pellis and Pellis point to laughter, rooted in the PLAY system, as a good example of how to deal with uncertainty. They explain:

From a functional point of view, laughter has been shown to activate the pleasure centers of the brain and induce a positive state in those laughing, and sometimes, even in those that witness others laughing. Not surprisingly, laughter is often used when confronting uncertain social situations, probably as a vehicle with which to induce a positive mood and avoid misunderstandings. However, humor, the major instigator of laughter, is also employed to reduce stress and facilitate bonding, as well as to gain status. Thus, using the "I was only joking" gambit is not unlike the "I was only playing" ploy. (pp. 142–143)

Laughter and play help us to negotiate our social relationships while managing our windows of tolerance.

I am confident that play will reemerge if enough of us make conscious choices about allowing both of our hemispheres to participate in solving the problems associated with a culture that appears to be losing its capacity to play. I am hopeful because of grass-roots innovators such as Marc Otto and his wife Melanya Helene who have developed a "Play after Play" theater/play program in Portland, Oregon, where children and their parents learn about the deep communicative nature of play. In a small theater, the audience sits around the edges of several large play mats to see a performance of a play—the dramatization of a traditional wisdom tale—by one or more professional actors. After the play, the actors (also trained play specialists) invite the children and their parents onto the play mats for a round or two of *real* play. This participatory play is physical, but the actors/play specialists consciously lead it as an experience of *connection through play*. The focus of their play is communication through "attuning to each child in the moment and modeling safe, gentle play." You can see a video of their play style with children by visiting their website (www.playafterplay.com) where you will find the following play intentions:

- Our play focuses on cooperation and empathy rather than on competition and resistance.
- Our play is rooted in safety and trust, and communicates kindness and belonging.
- Our play engages the whole child—all their senses and imagination.

181

- As play specialists, we are here to model safety and kindness in all moments and in all interactions. (www.playafterplay.com)

Although we might classify this kind of play as a commodity (because tickets are purchased for a performance), it is a wonderful example of *moving through our dilemma about play* rather than trying to return to the good old days. Although this play program needs to be purchased as a commodity, it goes beyond the kind of play that is packaged purely for entertainment and profit. Learning from *Play after Play* experiences, parents and children can take home new skills that they can incorporate into their daily lives, into the freedom of exploratory play with each other just for the sake of having fun, with an outcome of deepening connection. The availability of numerous programs like *Play after Play* could help us build the healthy brains that we need for a healthy society that prizes and wishes to pursue freedom through playful connection.

Beginning Again with the Legos

The Weston family did begin playing again at home after several sessions of Lego play in my office and several discussions with the parents about how play stops under circumstances of adversity (Sivy, 2010). We also talked about how play itself can help to relieve stress by consciously making a decision to reengage the ventral vagal "green light" of safety. The father's experience of recognizing how his own window of tolerance had narrowed due to financial stress, and how it had impacted his boys through their resonance circuits, helped him make a conscious decision about reengaging in playful activities with his family. Although it took about 6 months for the financial stress to diminish, they began to play again, and they later told me that their reengagement in playful activities, along with the neuroscience information, had had a calming effect on all of them.

PLAYING WITH PAINT

I want to conclude this book with a personal play story. I have never considered myself to be an artist, as in the kind of artist who paints beautiful canvases. My undergraduate degree is in music, however, and so I have always loved creative activities, and I have been curious about the visual arts for a long time. It's just that I knew, after my seventh-grade art class at school, that I would never be an artist—that is, until I met Donna Hanna-Chase, a professional artist, marriage and family therapist, colleague, mentor, and friend. Over the years, she and I have had a lot of discussions about art and especially about sand tray therapy. One day she was telling me about what it was like to be an art teacher. She said that one of the most difficult things about teaching students to do art is helping them let go of the need to paint a "beautiful flower," or a "landscape," or some other specific object. She said, "If I can just get them to put paint on the canvas, then I can teach them to do art."

In my naiveté, I said (to myself), "Well, I can do that!" Feeling safe with Donna, I said (out loud), "I'd like to learn to paint." Enthusiastically, she replied. "Great!" So we set up a time to go to a shared studio where she and other artists often gathered to paint together. When we arrived at the studio, she got out the watercolors and handed me a large (18" × 24"), beautiful piece of watercolor paper. I was pretty sure the paper was expensive because it was not like any other paper I have ever used for art. She showed me how to mix the colors and gave me a set of brushes.

Immediately, I froze! I had no idea how to begin, especially not on such an expensive piece of paper! Donna saw my hesitancy, and said, "Here, let me help." She took my large beautiful piece of paper and placed it carefully on the floor. She stepped on the paper, simultaneously pulling me gently onto the paper with her. She led me in a few "dance steps" on the paper, then, picking up the paper, she handed it back to me, and said, "Now you can paint." I was horrified. There were dirty footprints all over my beautiful piece of paper. "Oh, well," I thought, "I might as well use the paper. I'll just cover up the marks and then see what happens." I covered up the first footprint with a wide double stroke of blue—then another stoke of paint, and another. Soon I was playing and experimenting with lots of different colors, brushes, and shapes of all kinds. I was *just playing* with brushes and paint. It was such fun, and it satisfied something very deep inside.

Since that day I have painted numerous times, and I have always done it just for fun. I still don't think of myself as an artist (as in professional), but I do know that playing with paints is fun and deeply satisfying—just because. Sometimes when I get stuck for words, I just paint (just play). It is just what I need to find the words once more.

That's how I began to play again.

APPENDIX

Handouts

HANDOUT #1

MOTIVATIONAL* CIRCUITS IN THE BRAIN
Jaak Panksepp

ACTIVATED WHEN WE ARE **OUT OF CONNECTION** WITH SIGNIFICANT OTHERS	ACTIVATED WHEN WE ARE **IN CONNECTION** WITH SIGNIFICANT OTHERS
• RAGE (anger) • FEAR (anxiety) • PANIC/GRIEF (Separation Distress)	• CARE (nurturance) • LUST (sexual excitement) • PLAY (social joy)
• SEEKING (expectancy)	

*Panksepp sometimes uses the terms, *Emotional Systems* or *Affective Systems* to refer to these seven unique *Motivational Circuits.*

SEVEN PRIMARY EMOTIONAL SYSTEMS

NOTES FOR USE:

This diagram shows us seven primary emotional systems that lie deep in the brain (subcortical regions). They are arranged here to emphasize the importance of connectedness or disconnectedness in their activation. Panksepp calls these systems "ancestral tools for living" that we inherit at birth. These seven affective systems each have their own neural circuitry. The SEEKING circuit is the primary emotional-motivational circuit, impacting all of the other circuits except RAGE, which arises when SEEKING is thwarted. SEEKING is active when CARE, LUST, or PLAY emerge in conditions of safety and connection, and also active when FEAR and PANIC/GRIEF/Separation Distress emanate from the felt sense of being unsafe and disconnected from sources of support.

This chart also helps us to see that PLAY matters. Mother Nature did not create it just for fun and frivolity. The PLAY circuitry evolved, no doubt, because it gives us an important tool for helping to create the joy of social relationships.

More Information: See text, Chapter 1, pp. 7–9.

Sunderland, Margot (2006). *The science of parenting: How today's brain research can help you raise happy, emotionally balanced children.* New York, NY: DK Publishing.

HANDOUT #2

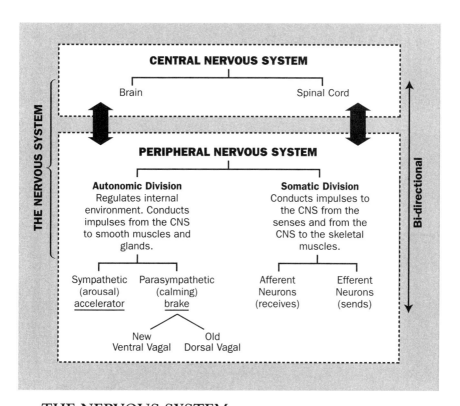

THE NERVOUS SYSTEM

NOTES FOR USE:

In this diagram we can see both the differentiating and the integrating parts of the nervous system. The two main divisions, the central nervous system (CNS) and the peripheral nervous system (PNS) connect with each other in a bi-directional manner. The messages that are sent back and forth between the CNS and the PNS help us to regulate incoming and outgoing stimuli and behavioral responses. Familiarity with this simple structure creates a foundation for understanding how PLAY functions in the nervous system from the perspective of the polyvagal theory (Porges, 2011). Infant and early childhood play, especially within nurturing relationships, provides positive affective experiences that are helpful in developing well-modulated nervous systems.

More Information: See text, Chapter 1, pp. 11–13.

HANDOUT #3

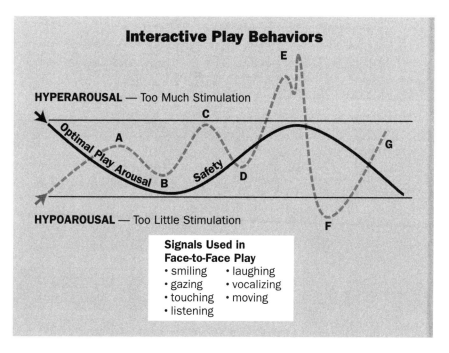

Interactive Play Behaviors

HYPERAROUSAL — Too Much Stimulation

Optimal Play Arousal

Safety

HYPOAROUSAL — Too Little Stimulation

A B C D E F G

Signals Used in Face-to-Face Play
- smiling
- laughing
- gazing
- vocalizing
- touching
- moving
- listening

INFANT PLAY IN THE NERVOUS SYSTEM

NOTES FOR USE:

This diagram provides a clear picture of what happens in early play between infants and mothering people. We can see the balancing of the accelerator (sympathetic) and the brakes (parasympathetic) during optimal play arousal. We also see what happens when the infant experiences too much stimulation (hyperarousal) or too little stimulation (hypoarousal). Almost any parent-infant play example, such as "peek-a-boo" or "I'm-gonna-getcha" will serve to illustrate how play helps the infant begin to manage this complicated nervous system within the safety of nurturing relationships with mothering people.

More Information: See text, pp. 23–25.

HANDOUT #4

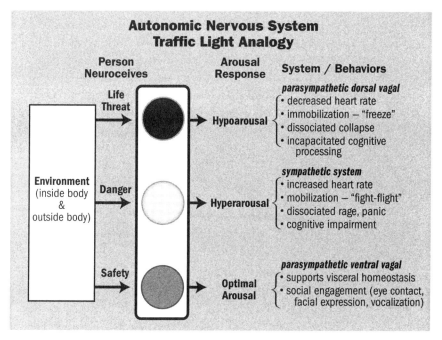

TRAFFIC LIGHT ANALOGY

NOTES FOR USE:

In conjunction with Handouts (p. 187 and p. 188), we can use this handout to build on the concept that the PLAY system helps us develop a nervous system that responds rapidly to the challenges of the environment (internally or externally). The traffic light is a good analogy for introducing the three branches of the autonomic nervous system in Porges' polyvagal theory: green (safety), yellow (danger), and red (life threatening). It is a hierarchical surveillance system that works without our conscious awareness to help us manage our biobehavioral quest for maintaining safety in connection with others. The System/Behaviors column gives us a clear visual for how lack of safety impairs or even dismantles our cognitive processing. With a well-developed PLAY system, it is often possible for us to come back into social engagement (optimal arousal) in a timely manner.

More Information: See text, Chapter 2, pp. 13–18.

HANDOUT #5

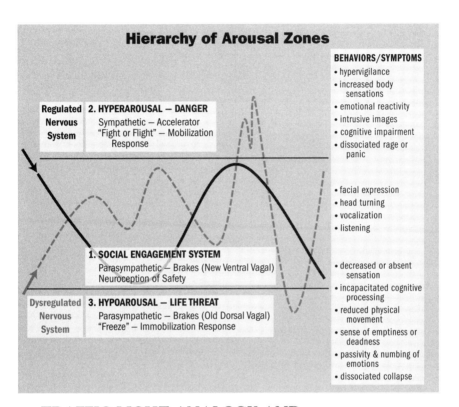

Hierarchy of Arousal Zones

BEHAVIORS/SYMPTOMS
- hypervigilance
- increased body sensations
- emotional reactivity
- intrusive images
- cognitive impairment
- dissociated rage or panic

- facial expression
- head turning
- vocalization
- listening

- decreased or absent sensation
- incapacitated cognitive processing
- reduced physical movement
- sense of emptiness or deadness
- passivity & numbing of emotions
- dissociated collapse

Regulated Nervous System

2. HYPERAROUSAL – DANGER
Sympathetic – Accelerator
"Fight or Flight" – Mobilization Response

1. SOCIAL ENGAGEMENT SYSTEM
Parasympathetic – Brakes (New Ventral Vagal)
Neuroception of Safety

Dysregulated Nervous System

3. HYPOAROUSAL – LIFE THREAT
Parasympathetic – Brakes (Old Dorsal Vagal)
"Freeze" – Immobilization Response

TRAFFIC LIGHT ANALOGY AND WINDOW OF TOLERANCE

NOTES FOR USE:

Combining the traffic light analogy (p. 189) and our diagram of optimal play arousal (p. 188), we can use this handout to show a more complete picture of the polyvagal theory (Porges, 2011) when we rearrange the green, yellow and red signals, with green (optimal) in the middle, yellow (caution) on top, and red (stop) on the bottom. Using the Behaviors/Symptoms column, we can learn how to observe when others are moving out of their social engagement systems giving us a gauge for monitoring and calibrating our own behaviors and interventions to help us restore social engagement and optimal cognitive functioning. This handout will be useful for introducing the concepts of the "Window of Tolerance" from trauma literature (Chapter 2, pp. 32–34) and the polyvagal definition of play (Chapter 2, pp. 34–36).

More Information: See text, Chapter 2, pp. 32–36.

HANDOUT #6

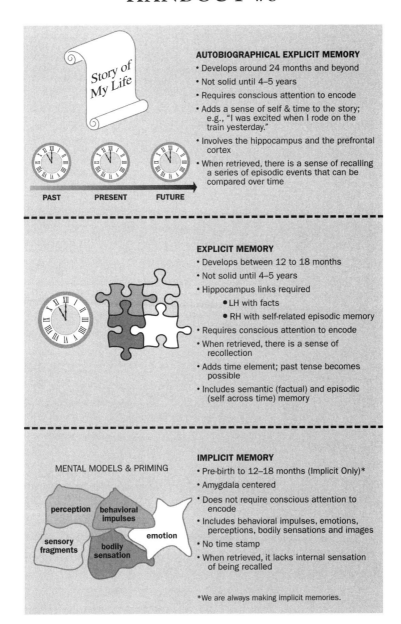

AUTOBIOGRAPHICAL EXPLICIT MEMORY
- Develops around 24 months and beyond
- Not solid until 4–5 years
- Requires conscious attention to encode
- Adds a sense of self & time to the story; e.g., "I was excited when I rode on the train yesterday."
- Involves the hippocampus and the prefrontal cortex
- When retrieved, there is a sense of recalling a series of episodic events that can be compared over time

PAST   PRESENT   FUTURE

EXPLICIT MEMORY
- Develops between 12 to 18 months
- Not solid until 4–5 years
- Hippocampus links required
  - LH with facts
  - RH with self-related episodic memory
- Requires conscious attention to encode
- When retrieved, there is a sense of recollection
- Adds time element; past tense becomes possible
- Includes semantic (factual) and episodic (self across time) memory

MENTAL MODELS & PRIMING

perception   behavioral impulses

sensory fragments   bodily sensation   emotion

IMPLICIT MEMORY
- Pre-birth to 12–18 months (Implicit Only)*
- Amygdala centered
- Does not require conscious attention to encode
- Includes behavioral impulses, emotions, perceptions, bodily sensations and images
- No time stamp
- When retrieved, it lacks internal sensation of being recalled

*We are always making implicit memories.

LEVELS OF MEMORY

NOTES FOR USE:

This chart gives us a visual of the differences in the two major ways the brain makes memories: implicit and explicit. We can see the hierarchical nature of the amygdala-centered implicit memories (bottom level) and the explicit memories (middle and top levels) that require hippocampal functioning. We are using a broken line between the types to indicate that there is a dynamic flow and potential integration among the levels. This image also provides us with an introduction to mental models and how positive affective experiences associated with early infant-parent play can be built into the memory system of the brain and mind.

More Information: See text, Chapter 5, pp. 82–88.

HANDOUT #7

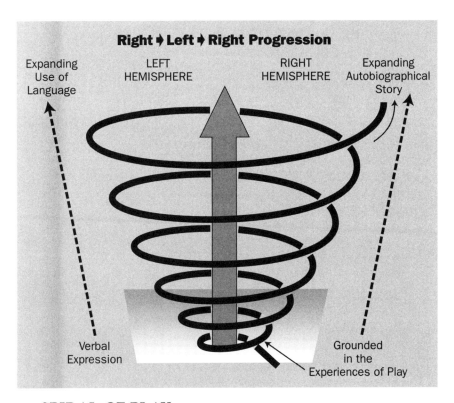

SPIRAL OF PLAY
NEUROBIOLOGY OF THE
STORYTELLING BRAIN

NOTES FOR USE:

This spiral of play shows us how storytelling integrates our embodied experiences in the world (right hemisphere) with our love for telling the stories (left hemisphere) that we continuously experience (lived experiences in the right hemisphere) as we interact with our environments. The spiral connects our hemispheres irreversibly in ever-increasing levels of integration.

More Information: See text, Chapter 9, pp. 119–126.
See text, Chapter 12, pp. 176–178.

HANDOUT #8

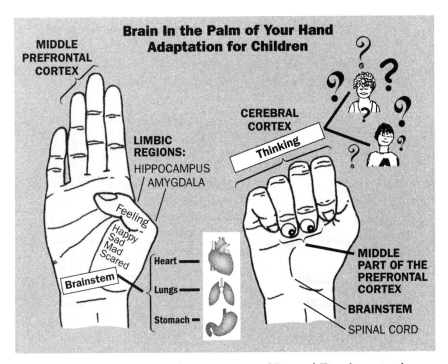

Adapted from *Mindsight: The New Science of Personal Transformation,* by Daniel J. Siegel, M.D. (2012), p.15.

BRAIN IN THE PALM OF YOUR HAND ADAPTATION FOR CHILDREN

NOTES FOR USE:

This handout is for parents, children, and teachers showing a play exercise that helps with the terminology of the brain, using Daniel Siegel's well-known "Brain in the Palm of Your Hand." Using face paints or washable markers, ask children (or children and parents) to decorate their hands, and even their arms, painting whatever they like to represent the different parts of the brain (brain stem, limbic system and cortex). Ask them to paint something that represents for them the heart and lungs and stomach on the base of their palms to show how the brain stem helps us regulate some things automatically. Then ask them to paint feelings on their thumbs and in the palms of their hands for the limbic system, and then something to represent the thinking and relating parts of the prefrontal cortex on their knuckles. Some children may get creative and paint spinal cords on their wrists or eyes on their fingernails. When they are finished painting, they will enjoy playing with the concept of "flipping our lids" as they open and close their fingers over their thumbs, simulating the movement in and out of dysregulation. Children especially love doing this exercise with their parents.

This play exercise can be done individually (painting on one's own hand, or in relational pairs (painting on each other's hands). After painting, each person gets to tell the story of the "Brain in the Palm of Your Hand."

More Information: See text, Chapter 11, pp. 154–156.

Siegel, D., & Bryson, T. (2011) *The whole-brain child: Revolutionary strategies to nurture your child's mind*. New York, NY: Delacorte Press.

REFERENCES

Ainsworth, M. D. S., Blehar, J. C., Waters, E., & Wall, S. (1978). *Patterns of attachment: A psychological study of the strange situation*. Hillsdale, NJ: Erlbaum.

Badenoch, B. (2008). *Being a brain-wise therapist: A practical guide to interpersonal neurobiology*. New York, NY: Norton.

Badenoch, B. (2011). *The brain-savvy therapist's workbook*. New York, NY: Norton.

Baer, R. A. (Ed.). (2006). *Mindfulness-based treatment approaches: Clinician's guide to evidence base and applications*. Burlington, MA: Academic Press.

Baer, R. A., Smith, G. T., Hopkins, J., Krietemeyer, J., & Toney, L. (2006). Using self-report assessment methods to explore facets of mindfulness. *Assessment, 13*(1), 27–45.

Beckoff, M., & Byers, J. (1998). *Animal play: Evolutionay, comparative, and ecological perspectives*. New York, NY: Cambridge University Press.

Berk, L. E., & Meyers, A. B. (2013). The role of make-believe play in the development of executive function: Status of research and future directions. *American Journal of Play, 6*(1), 98–110.

Bodrova, E., Germeroth, C., & Leong, D. J. (2013). Play and self-regulation: Lessons from Vygotsky. *American Journal of Play, 6*(1), 111–123.

Bowlby, J. (1953). *Child care and the growth of love*. London: Penguin Books.

Bowlby, J. (1969). *Attachment and loss: Vol. 1. Attachment*. New York, NY: Basic Books.

Brown, S., & Vaughan, C. (2009). *Play: How it shapes the brain, opens the imagination, and invigorates the soul*. New York, NY: Avery (Penguin Group).

Damasio, A. (1999). *The feeling of what happens: The body and emotion in the making of consciousness*. San Diego, CA: Harcourt.

Damasio, A. (2010). *Self comes to mind: Constructing the conscious mind*. New York, NY: Random House.

Dobbs, D. (2006, April/May). Human see, human, do. *Scientific American Mind*, 22–27, Vol. 294.

Ecker, B., Ticic, R., Hulley, L., & Neimeyer, R. A. (2012). *Unlocking the emotional brain: Eliminating symptoms at their roots using memory reconsolidation.* New York, NY: Routledge.

Gauntlett, D. (2007). *Creative explorations: New approaches to identities and audiences.* New York, NY: Routledge.

Gray, P. (2011). The decline of play and the rise of psychopathology in children and adolescents. *American Journal of Play, 3*(4), 443–463.

Greenland, S. K. (2010). *The mindful child: How to help your child manage stress and become happier, kinder, and more compassionate.* New York, NY: Free Press.

Gusnard, D. A., & Raichle, M. E. (2001). Searching for a baseline: Functional imaging and the resting human brain. *National Review of Neuroscience, 2,* 685–694.

Harlow, H. (1962). The heterosexual affection system in monkeys. *American Psychologist, 17,* 1–9.

Hawkins, J., & Blakeslee, S. (2004). *On intelligence: How a new understanding of the brain will lead to the creation of truly intelligent machines.* New York, NY: Times Books.

Heath, R. (1996). *Exploring the mind–body relationship.* Baton Rouge, LA: Moran Printing.

Hebb, D. O. (1949). *The organization of behavior: A neuropsychological theory.* New York, NY: Wiley.

Higgins-Klein, D. (2013). *Mindfulness-based play-family therapy: Theory and practice.* New York, NY: Norton.

Huizinga, J. (1955). *Homo ludens: A study of the play element in culture.* Boston, MA: Beacon Press.

Jung, C. (1969). *The collected works of C. G. Jung. Vol. 8. The structure and dynamics of the psyche* (2nd ed.). Princeton, NJ: Princeton University Press.

Jung, C. (1989). *Memories, dreams, reflections.* New York, NY: Vintage Books. (Original work published 1961)

Kalff, Dora (1980). *Sandplay: A psychotherapeutic approach to the psyche.* Boston, MA: Sigo Press.

Kalff, Dora (2003). *Sandplay: A psychotherapeutic approach to the psyche.* Cloverdale, CA: Temenos Press. (Original work published 1980)

Kestly, T. (2010). Group sandplay in elementary schools. In A. Drewes & C. Schaefer (Eds.), *School-based play therapy* (pp. 257–281). New York, NY: Wiley.

Lazar, S. W., Kerr, C. E., Wasserman, R. H., Gray, J. R., Greve, D. N., Treadway, M. T., et al. (2005). Meditation experience is associated with increased cortical thickness. *NeuroReport, 16*(17), 1893–1897.

LeDoux, J. E. (1996). *The emotional brain.* New York, NY: Simon & Schuster.

Lillard, A. S., Lerner, M. D., Hopkins, E. J., Dore, R. A., Smith, E. D., &

Palmquist, C. M. (2013). The impact of pretend play on children's development: A review of the evidence. *Psychological Bulletin, 139,* 1–34.

Lowenfeld, M. (1993). *Understanding children's sandplay: Lowenfeld's World Technique.* Cambridge, Great Britain: Margaret Lowenfeld Trust. (Original work published 1979)

Mahler, M., Pine, F., & Bergman, A. (1975). *The psychological birth of an infant.* New York, NY: Basic Books.

Main, M. (1996). Introduction to the special section on attachment and psychopathology: 2. Overview of the field of attachment. *Journal of Consulting and Clinical Psychology, 64,* 237–243.

Main, M. (2000). The Adult Attachment Interview: Fear, Attention, Safety, and Discourse Processes. *Journal of the American Psychoanalytic Association, 48,* 1055–1096.

Main, M., & Hesse, E. (1999). Second-generation effects of unresolved trauma in non-maltreating parents: Dissociated, frightened, and threatening parental behavior. *Psychoanalytic Inquiry, 19,* 481–540.

Marks-Tarlow, T. (2012). *Clinical intuition in psychotherapy: The neurobiology of embodied response.* New York, NY: Norton.

McGilchrist, I. (2009). *The master and his emissary: The divided brain and the making of the Western world.* New Haven, CT: Yale University Press.

Ogden, P., Minton, K., & Pain, C. (2006). *Trauma and the body: A sensorimotor approach to psychotherapy.* New York, NY: Norton.

Otto, M. (2010, Autumn/Winter). A meditation on play. *Connections & Reflections: The GAINS Quarterly,* 71–75.

Panksepp, J. (1985). Mood changes. *Handbook of clinical neurology: Vol. 1. Clinical neuropsychology* (pp. 271–285). Amsterdam: Elsevier Science Publishers. New York, NY: Norton.

Panksepp, J. (1998). *Affective neuroscience: The foundations of human and animal emotions.* New York, NY: Oxford University Press.

Panksepp, J. (2005). Affective consciousness: Core emotional feelings in animals and humans. *Consciousness & Cognition, 14,* 19–69.

Panksepp, J. (2007). Can PLAY diminish ADHD and facilitate the construction of the social brain? *Journal of the Canadian Academy of Child and Adolescent Psychiatry, 16*(2), 57–66.

Panksepp, J. (2008). Play, ADHD, and the construction of the social brain: Should the first class each day be recess? *American Journal of Play, 1*(1), 55–79.

Panksepp, J. (2009). Brain emotional systems and qualities of mental life: From animal models of affect to implications for psychotherapeutics. In D. Fosha, D. Siegel, & M. Solomon (Eds.), *The healing power of emotion: Affective neuroscience, development, and clinical practice* (pp. 1–26). New York, NY: Norton.

Panksepp, J. (2010). Science of the brain as a gateway to understanding play: An interview with Jaak Panksepp. *American Journal of Play, 2*(3), 245–277.

Panksepp, J. (2011). Cross-species affective neuroscience decoding of the primal affective experiences of humans and related animals. *PLoS One, 6*(9), e21236. doi:10.1371/journal.pone.0021236

Panksepp, J., & Biven, L. (2012). *The archaeology of mind: Neuroevolutionary origins of human emotions.* New York, NY: Norton.

Pellegrini, A. D. (2005). *Recess: Its role in education and development.* Mahwah, NJ: Erlbaum.

Pellegrini, A. D. (2008). The recess debate: A disjuncture between educational policy and scientific research. *American Journal of Play, 1*(2), 181–191.

Pellegrini, A. D., & Bohm-Gettler, C. M. (2013). The benefits of recess in primary school. *Scholarpedia, 8*(2), 30448.

Pellis, S., & Pellis, V. (2009). *The playful brain: Venturing to the limits of neuroscience.* New York, NY: Oneworld Publications.

Pellis, M., Pellis, V., & Bell, H. C. (2010). The function of play in the development of the social brain. *American Journal of Play, 2*(3), 278–296.

Perry, B. (1997). Incubated in terror: Neurodevelopmental factors in the "cycle of violence." In J. Osofsky (Ed.), *Children, youth, and violence: The search for solutions* (pp. 124–148). New York, NY: Guilford Press.

Perry, B. (2009). Examining child maltreatment through a neurodevelopmental lens: Clinical applications of the neurosequential model of therapeutics. *Journal of Loss and Trauma, 14*, 240–255.

Perry, B., & Szalavitz, M. (2006). *The boy who was raised as a dog: What traumatized children teach us about loss, love, and healing.* New York, NY: Basic Books.

Porges, S. (2009). Reciprocal influences between body and brain in the perception and expression of affect: A polyvagal perspective. In D. Fosha, D. Siegel, & M. Solomon (Eds.), *The healing power of emotion: Affective neuroscience, development, and clinical practice* (pp. 27–54). New York, NY: Norton.

Porges, S. (2011). *The polyvagal theory: Neurophysiological foundations of emotions, attachment, communication, and self-regulation.* New York: Norton.

Porges, S. (2012). *Negotiating safe places in therapeutic settings and social relationships: A polyvagal perspective.* Brain–Body Center, University of Illinois at Chicago.

Porges, S., & Carter, S. (2010). *The love code: Social engagement and social bonding.* http://www.eabp.org/pdf/The_Polyvagal_Theory_S_Porges.pdf

Raichle, M. (2010). The brain's dark energy. *Scientific American, 302*(3), 44–49.

Ramstetter, C. L., Murray, R., & Garner, A. S. (2010). The crucial role of recess in schools. *Journal of School Health, 80*(11), 517–526.

Rifkin, J. (2000). *The age of access: The new culture of hypercapitalism where all of life is a paid-for experience*. New York, NY: Tarcher/Putnam.

Rogers, F. (1994). *You are special*. New York, NY: Viking (Penguin Group).

Schore, A. N. (1994). *Affect regulation and the origin of the self: The neurobiology of emotional development*. Hillsdale, NJ: Erlbaum.

Schore, A. N. (2009). Right-brain affect regulation: An essential mechanism of development, trauma, dissociation, and psychotherapy. In D. Fosha, D. J. Siegel, & M. Solomon (Eds.), *The healing power of emotion: Affective neuroscience, development and clinical practice* (pp. 112–144). New York, NY: Norton.

Schore, A. N. (2012). *The science of the art of psychotherapy*. New York, NY: Norton.

Schore, A. N., & Newton, R. (2011). Using regulation theory to guide clinical assessments of mother-infant attachment relationships. In Schore, A. N. (Ed.), *The science of the art of psychotherapy*. New York: NY: Norton.

Semple, R. J., & Lee, J. (2011). *Mindfulness-based cognitive therapy for anxious children: A manual for treating childhood anxiety*. Oakland, CA: New Harbinger.

Semple, R. J., Lee, J., & Miller, L. F. (2006). Mindfulness-based cognitive therapy for children. In R. A. Baer (Ed.), *Mindfulness-based treatment approaches: Clinician's guide to evidence base and applications*. Burlington, MA: Academic Press.

Siegel, D. J. (1999). *The developing mind: How relationships and the brain interact to shape who we are*. New York, NY: Guilford Press.

Siegel, D. J. (2006). An interpersonal neurobiology approach to psychotherapy: Awareness, mirror neurons, and neural plasticity in the development of well-being. *Psychiatric Annals, 36*(4), 247–258.

Siegel, D. J. (2007). *The mindful brain: Reflection and attunement in the cultivation of well-being*. New York, NY: Norton.

Siegel, D. J. (2010). *Mindsight: The new science of personal transformation*. New York, NY: Bantam Books.

Siegel, D. J. (2012). *The developing mind: How relationships and the brain interact to shape who we are* (2nd ed.). New York, NY: Guilford Press.

Siegel, D. J., & Bryson, T. P. (2011). *The whole-brain child: 12 revolutionary strategies to nurture your child's developing mind*. New York, NY: Delacorte Press.

Siegel, D. J., & Hartzell, M. (2003). *Parenting from the inside out: How a deeper self-understanding can help you raise children who thrive*. New York, NY: Tacher/Penguin.

Sivy, S. M. (2010). Play and adversity: How the playful mammalian brain withstands threats and anxieties. *American Journal of Play, 2*(3), 297–314.

Spitz, R. A., & Wolf, K. M. (1946). Anaclitic depression: An inquiry into the genesis of psychiatric conditions in early childhood. *Psychoanalytic Study of the Child, 2,* 313–342.

Stern, D. N. (2002). *The first relationship: Infant and mother.* Cambridge, MA: Harvard University Press. (Original work published 1977)

Sunderland, M. (2006). *The science of parenting: How today's brain research can help you raise happy, emotionally balanced children.* New York, NY: DK Publishing.

Vaillant, G. E. (2002). *Aging well.* Boston: Little, Brown.

Wheatley-Crosbie, J. R. (2006). Healing traumatic reenactment: Psyche's return from soma's underworld. *USA Body Psychotherapy Journal, 5,* 10–28.

Winnicott, D. W. (1971/2005). *Playing and reality* (new revised edition). New York, NY: Tavistock Publications.

INDEX